For Emilia Lanier (Bassano) 1569-1645

Morgan Lloyd Malcolm

EMILIA

OBERON BOOKS
LONDON

WWW.OBERONBOOKS.COM

First published in 2018 by Oberon Books Ltd
521 Caledonian Road, London N7 9RH
Tel: +44 (0) 20 7607 3637 / Fax: +44 (0) 20 7607 3629
e-mail: info@oberonbooks.com
www.oberonbooks.com

A catalogue record for this book is available from the British Library.

PB ISBN: 9781786824813
E ISBN: 9781786824820

Cover image: Dewynters

Contents

I want to say thank you to Michelle Terry for giving me this opportunity. Without her passion and faith this project would never have begun. I want to say thank you to Nicole Charles for being my co-conspirator and dreamer. I feel so lucky to have made this with you. I want to say thank you for Kate, Eleanor, Eileen and Nica and your brilliant teams who saw what we made at the Globe and brought it to the beautiful Vaudeville Theatre. Thank you for believing in us. I want to say thank you to all the incredible women in the cast and crew and creative team. You have grabbed this opportunity with both hands and put so much of your hearts and beautiful souls into this piece and it shows. I have loved every moment of working with you. To the original cast and crew and everyone at the Globe, I will always be indebted to the work you put in and the love you gave. I feel like we began a family which will only grow and grow. Thank you to Georgina and Hannah at David Higham Associates, to everyone at Oberon, to my friends and my family. I also want to say thank you to the huge community both online and off who have supported and championed this play and everything we're trying to do; your enthusiasm helped get us to the west end! And finally thank you to Emilia Bassano whose words sit within all of us now. We all think you're amazing and we hope you like what we have made.

A note on the text

This play was written to be performed by an all female cast of diverse women. It would not be the same play if this is ignored. If being performed in a school where it is impossible to adhere to this then please cast against the 'usual type'. Be bold.

This play was also written to challenge the notion that a play about a person needs to be a vehicle for one actress. This is very much an ensemble piece hence the three Emilias. It takes place in several time zones at one time. It isn't an accurate representation of Renaissance England, it isn't a historical representation. It is a memory, a dream, a feeling of her.

CHARACTERS (grouped in the doubling made in the original production. However if you have a larger group of actresses do share these parts out more. Or if you see better doubling due to specific skills of your actresses do mix them up. This is just a guide.)

This production had new music composed by Luisa Gerstein and the vibe and style is intrinsic to the piece.

Characters

EMILIA1

EMILIA2

EMILIA3

The three Emilias represent the
three ages of her.

MARGARET JOHNSON /
MARY SIDNEY / HESTER

SUSAN BERTIE THE COUNTESS
OF KENT / MARY / BOB

LADY HELENA / LORD HOWARD / EVE

LADY CORDELIA / FLORA

LADY KATHERINE / DESDEMONA (Othello)

LORD THOMAS HOWARD / JUDITH / PRIEST

LORD COLLINS / LADY ANNE / DAVE

LORD ALPHONSO LANIER / EMILIA (Othello)

WILLIAM SHAKESPEARE / MAN 2

LADY MARGARET CLIFFORD /
MIDWIFE / MAN 1

THE MUSES

Everyone except EMILIA3 is a Muse. They play
every other character in the play. The muses are
the embodiment of Emilia's will. It is up to you
how you show this.

Emilia was first performed at the Globe Theatre on 10 August 2018. The cast was as follows:

LADY KATHERINE HOWARD	Nadia Albina
LADY MARY SIDNEY	Anna Andresen
LADY ANNE CLIFFORD	Shiloh Coke
EMILIA 1	Leah Harvey
COUNTESS OF KENT / MARY	Jenni Maitland
EMILIA 3	Clare Perkins
LORD HENRY CAREY / JUDITH	Carolyn Pickles
EMILIA 2	Vinette Robinson
LORD THOMAS HOWARD / HESTER	Sophie Russell
LADY CORDELIA / FLORA	Sarah Seggari
LADY MARGARET CLIFFORD	Sophie Stone
WILLIAM SHAKESPEARE	Charity Wakefield
ALPHONSO LANIER	Amanda Wilkin
MUSICAL DIRECTOR / SHAWMS / RECORDERS / DULCIANS / BAGPIPES	Emily Baines
SACKBUT / GUITAR	Elinor Chambers
DRUMS / PERCUSSION	Calie Hough
SHAWMS / RECORDERS	Sarah Humphrys
SHAWMS / RECORDERS / BAGPIPES / VIOLIN	Sharon Lindo

Creatives

Writer	Morgan Lloyd Malcolm
Director	Nicole Charles
Designer	Jo Scotcher
Assistant Director	Anna Dirckinck-Holmfeld
Composer	Bill Barclay
Choreographer and Movement Direction	Anna Morrisey
Costume Supervisor	Lydia Crimp
Physical Comedy Director	Joe Dieffenbacher
Fight Directors	Rachel Bown-Williams and Ruth Cooper-Brown of Rc-Annie Ltd
Voice Coach	Tess Dignan
Production Manager	Fay Powell Thomas
Stage Manager	Liz Isaac
Deputy Stage Manager	Carol Pestridge
Assistant Stage Managers	Aislinn Jackson, Anthony Papamichael

Emilia transferred to Vaudeville Theatre, London and was first performed on 8 March 2019. The cast was as follows:

LADY KATHERINE HOWARD / DESDEMONA / RIVER WOMAN	Nadia Albina
LADY MARY SIDNEY / MARGARET JOHNSON / HESTER	Anna Andresen
ENSEMBLE / MUSICIAN	Christina Bloom
LORD THOMAS HOWARD / EVE/LADY HELENA	Jackie Clune
EMILIA 1	Saffron Coomber
ENSEMBLE	Lauren Drennan
ENSEMBLE	Eva Fontaine
ENSEMBLE	Cora Kirk
EMILIA 2	Adelle Leonce
COUNTESS OF KENT / MARY / BOB	Jenni Maitland
EMILIA 3	Clare Perkins
LORD HENRY CAREY / JUDITH /PRIEST	Carolyn Pickles
LADY CORDELIA / FLORA	Sarah Seggari
LADY MARGARET CLIFFORD /MIDWIFE / MAN 1/ PRIEST 2 / RIVER WOMAN	Sophie Stone
ENSEMBLE / MUSICIAN	Samantha Sutherland
WILLIAM SHAKESPEARE / MAN 2 / RIVER WOMAN	Charity Wakefield
ALPHONSO LANIER/ RIVER WOMAN / EMILIA IN OTHELLO	Amanda Wilkin
LADY ANNE CLIFFORD / LORD COLLINS / DAVE / RIVER WOMAN	Tanika Yearwood

Creatives

Writer	Morgan Lloyd Malcolm
Director	Nicole Charles
Designer	Joanna Scotcher
Lighting Designer	Zoe Spurr
Sound Designer	Emma Laxton
Choreographer and Movement Direction	Anna Morrissey
Composer	Luisa Gerstein
Musical Director	Yshani Perinpanayagam
Voice Coach	Tess Dignan
Costume Supervisor	Sian Harris
Wigs Supervisor	Jessica Plews
Assistant Director	Rafaella Marcus
Assistant Designer	Amelia Jane Hankin
Assistant Choreographer	Christina Fulcher (Attachment to the production from Central School of Speech and Drama)
Associate Lighting Designer	Anna Reddyhoff
Fight Directors	Rachel Brown-Williams and Ruth Cooper Brown of RC-Annie Ltd
Production Manager	Sacha Milroy
Company Stage Manager	Rosie Gilbert
Deputy Stage Manager	Carol Pestridge
Assistant Stage Managers	Sophie Macfadyen and Sarah-Linn Taylor

It was produced by Eleanor Lloyd, Kate Pakenham, Nica Burns and Eilene Davidson.

Prologue

Present Day. EMILIA3 makes her way down through the auditorium and towards the stage. She steps up onto the stage, standing in front of the cloth. She is holding a copy of a book called 'Sex And Society In Shakespeare's Age – Simon Forman The Astrologer' by AL Rowse. She stands for a moment taking in the audience and space. She flicks the book open and begins to read snippets from it.

EMILIA3: "Emilia, daughter of Baptista Bassano and Margaret Johnson...married to a Lanier...paramour to my old Lord Hunsdon that was Lord Chamberlain...maintained in great pomp. She is high-minded...She was very brave in youth... She hath many false conceptions...She hath been favoured much of her Majesty and of many noblemen...She is now very needy, in debt...(and) if I go to Lanier this night or tomorrow, whether she will receive me and whether I shall be welcome to 'halek'.

EMILIA3 looks up to acknowledge this word. She mouths the word 'fuck'.

...she is or will be a harlot...She was familiar and friendly... but only she would not 'halek'...

Another look.

She was a whore and dealt evil with him" Simon Forman, the astrologer, wrote this.

She stops. She closes the book. She takes a deep breath.

"She was a whore"

She kisses her teeth and throws the book away. Deep breath.

For centuries these are the words they have used to describe me. Not anymore... I am Emilia.

She is joined by EMILIA2 and EMILIA3 on stage.

We are Emilia

They are joined by all the other women.

We are only as powerful as the stories we tell. We have not always been able to tell them. Time to listen!

The music kicks in, the front cloth rises and the women invade the stage. The music slows to become the funeral music and EMILIA1 singing Durme Durme at her father's funeral.

Here we are where all good stories must start: death.

As EMILIA1 sings MARGARET JOHNSON and PRIEST enter. This is the funeral of Baptista Bassano, EMILIA's father. The congregation listens to EMILIA1 sing. During, SUSAN BERTIE enters, seen by MARGARET.

EMILIA1: *(Singing.)* Durme, durme, querido hijico
durme sin ansia y dolor
cerra tus chicos ojicos
durme, durme con savor.
Cerra tus lindos ojicos
durme, durme con savor.

MARGARET gestures to EMILIA1 to come with her and the PRIEST.

I've written something to honour Papa. Can I read it?

MARGARET JOHNSON: You absolutely cannot!

EMILIA1 ignores her. Over the following MARGARET is very aware that SUSAN BERTIE is watching.

EMILIA1: *(Reading.)* Sweet holy rivers, pure celestiall springs
Proceeding from the fountaine of our life;
Swift sugred currents that salvation brings,
Cleare chrystall streames, purging all sinne and strife,
Faire floods, where souls do bathe their snow-white wings,
Before they flie to true eternall life:

2

Such sweet nectar and ambrosia, food of saints
Which, whoso tasteth, never after faints.

(To MARGARET.) Don't be angry.

SUSAN BERTIE: Let her do whatever she needs to do. What was it you just recited?

EMILIA1: I wrote it myself.

SUSAN BERTIE: Christ!

MARGARET JOHNSON: I can only apologise Countess.

SUSAN BERTIE: *(Interrupting.)* She shows great promise. Margaret I too lost my husband and I know the great fear that strikes into our hearts. My offer still stands. I'll look after her well and her introduction to court will be assured. The Queen has already requested my presence several times. I'm well placed to place her well. What do you say?

EMILIA1 runs to MARGARET and hangs off her skirt.

EMILIA1: Mama no!

MARGARET JOHNSON: Your father's left us with nothing. My dear Countess as you can see she is no delicate creature to be moulded

(To Emilia.)

Get up!

(To the Countess.)

She is wild and boisterous. Her father indulged in her the abandon of her heritage. She won't be tamed.

SUSAN BERTIE: I am well accustomed to the challenges of young ladies. I'm sure I can handle her. Shall we discuss the terms?

3

EMILIA1: No!

She sinks to her knees as MARGARET and SUSAN step away to speak. As EMILIA3 speaks the following we see EMILIA1 come to terms with her leaving. SUSAN BERTIE beckons her to leave with her. She embraces her mother MARGARET and they make the journey to BERTIE's home. We see MARGARET hiding her sadness from her daughter.

EMILIA3: Like a seed pressed down firmly in the soil, covered and left. Something laid root in me. I did not know it then but I know it now. In my travelling family of musicians I was the latest in a long line of uprooted growth, floating towards somewhere to settle. We had come to this island like so many seeking shelter and purpose and we had found it. My father and his brothers were revered in the court for their musicianship. We knew our luck. But we still felt the notion of our otherness. Our differences. We thought we were part of their world but it is an easy fall when you can no longer pay your way. I was only seven, I had to go.

ACT 1

SCENE 1

SUSAN BERTIE: Cheer up Emilia for godsake. You're one of the lucky ones. You will be afforded the very best of education but most importantly how to present and thrive in court. How to find yourself that coveted prize of a rich and powerful man who will keep you in comfort for all your days. For what else does a young woman want? What else does a young woman need? What else could be as important to you as this?

She sweeps off. EMILIA1 speaks to us.

EMILIA1: My voice. My voice feels too loud in here. I must try to whisper more. Though sometimes I can't help but scream! Shout! But I mustn't. I can't. My breath feels shallower than before. It's being contained. I'm changing. I'm being changed. Metamorphosis. Eight years. To go from child to woman. I must try to only speak when I'm asked. No screeching. No jumping about. I'm a young lady now. This is what I've learnt. You see? I can be tamed. I know now that as I grow I must also shrink. I must not take up too much space. If I am to marry well I need to practice these tricks to hush my whole being so that I am only seen when needed. This I have learnt. This I am to practice. This. Silence. Of being. This. And yet...

The COUNTESS enters loudly.

SUSAN BERTIE: Emilia my girl put down your studies we've got guests. If you are to be introduced to court as a young lady, you will need armour. Not just for your body – that's what the corsets are for- but for you my darling. What is both a woman's greatest shield and most devastating weapon?

EMILIA1: You mean our...?

She points towards her vagina.

SUSAN BERTIE: No! Dear lord have I taught you nothing? That's your meal ticket. I'm talking about your protection. LADIES!

EMILIA3 sends the women on.

To survive we protect each other. These young ladies will be your strength. And you will be theirs. Lady Helena.

LADY HELENA: Charmed.

SUSAN BERTIE: Lady Katherine

LADY KATHERINE: Charmed.

SUSAN BERTIE: And Lady Cordelia

LADY CORDELIA: Alright?

EMILIA1: Hello.

SUSAN BERTIE: They are here to learn with you. And over the next few years you'll become quite the regular fixture in court with these young ladies. I'll leave you to get acquainted. But prepare yourself for your first lesson together and I will return anon.

She leaves.

LADY HELENA: Oh thank god she's gone!

LADY CORDELIA: And now she has we can finally...

(She hoiks her skirts up and adjusts her underclothes.)

...oh thank the good lord for that; it was going up my bum! Emilia, it's so nice to finally meet you.

EMILIA1: Have you yet visited court?

LADY HELENA: Heavens no! I'm so nervous! You have natural beauty on your side – It's not easy for those of us who have to work harder on our outward appearance such as our dear, poor Lady Katherine here.

LADY KATHERINE: You better watch your mouth!

LADY HELENA: *(Pointing at her bosom.)* I'm just saying – you might be needing a little uplift because you're losing altitude in your old age.

LADY KATHERINE: I'm sixteen!

LADY HELENA: Which makes it all the more urgent.

LADY KATHERINE: You come at me one more time and I swear I'll...

LADY HELENA: You'll what? Throw your needle work at me? Read me some latin?

LADY KATHERINE: I'm not the one who should be worried Helena. I've never met anyone so ill suited to court – they'll laugh you out of there. I wouldn't be surprised if the Countess sent you home before you embarrass her.

LADY CORDELIA: Ladies! Dear lord. This is not becoming of our breeding.

LADY KATHERINE: Speaking of breeding – what's yours?

EMILIA1: Pardon?

LADY KATHERINE: Where are you from?

EMILIA1: London.

LADY KATHERINE: No. Where. Are. You. From?

EMILIA1: I. Am. From. London.

LADY KATHERINE: But you don't look like us.

EMILIA1: Is this your first time in London?

LADY KATHERINE: No I've been before!

LADY CORDELIA: Don't lie! She's born and bred in the shires and she's as clueless as the sheep her father owns.

LADY KATHERINE: Not true! I've travelled.

EMILIA1: Well if you had then you would know that London doesn't ascribe to just one type of person. It envelopes and welcomes all kinds. My family hark from over the sea...

LADY KATHERINE: I knew it! My father said that we were being inundated with families like yours. Fleeing wars, men migrating for work. Craftsmen are furious. Coming over here to take their work. That's what they're saying. You... It's a real problem, that's what my father said.

EMILIA1: Bet he's fun at parties. I cannot speak for other families but as musicians of the court we have been respected and revered for long enough to earn our place here. It is by our virtues that we are judged not our heritage and my family have proved themselves tenfold. I don't need to answer to you. Or your father and his questionable opinions about human beings rightfully seeking new lives.

LADY KATHERINE: Whatever. But all the virtue in the world will mean nothing if you walk into court as you are now. Do you know how to dance?

EMILIA1: Some.

LADY KATHERINE: Well you need to know them all.

The COUNTESS returns.

SUSAN BERTIE: Ladies!

LADY KATHERINE: You're lucky – the Countess is the best teacher around.

SUSAN BERTIE: We have the latest dance to learn girls! Chairs! Also we must spruce you and pluck you, tighten and rouge you to within an inch of your pretty little lives. We have a lot of hard work ahead of us my darlings but by the end of it you'll be in possession of the best bloody husbands the Court has to offer. Ladies – Are you ready to SLAY?

MUSIC. SUSAN BERTIE teaches the girls a dance that involves important lessons on etiquette.

Rise...and we're travelling....gliding...innocence...
seduction...coy...amused...listening faces...he's talking....
still talking...STILL talking...he's cracked a joke!....it's not funny. Practical assesment! Lady Katherine, hanky drop.

She drops a hanky and LADY KATHERINE daintily picks it up.

Steady.... Lovely. Emilia! Book walk.

EMILIA1 puts a book on her head and starts to walk,

Slowly... Good. Lady Cordelia, smile!

LADY CORDELIA gives her best smile.

Perfect! Lady Helena, solo dance.

(She demonstrates.)

Step, scissor scissor. Step, scissor scissor. Step, scissor scissor. Step, scissor scissor. And GO!

LADY HELENA attempts this and fails.

(To HELENA.) You're not ready for court. Go and practice alone. GO!

LADY HELENA exits.

Ladies! Re-form!

They dance.

Ladies, the men are waiting – time to be introduced to court!

Court life. MUSIC. Men arrive. They're on the prowl. This should be a dance in which the men display their 'attributes' – it should be very funny. The girls join others vying for attention. It's predatory and EMILIA1 finds it hard to engage – despite being the one getting the most attention. Time passes...

SCENE 2

EMILIA1 is busy scribbling in her note book and yet is still the main point of interest for the men (she does not notice them). LADY KATHERINE and LADY CORDELIA can see this and are getting frustrated.

EMILIA1: Cordelia, I've written a new sonnet. Would you like to hear it?

LADY CORDELIA: No! The last one was most saucy and I felt terribly flustered after hearing it.

LADY KATHERINE: I'll hear it.

LADY CORDELIA: Katherine! Stop it!

LADY KATHERINE: Why not? The more disreputable she becomes by writing like she's a man the less men will be interested and the more will be left for us.

LADY CORDELIA: Don't encourage her!

LADY KATHERINE: We need to level the playing field Cordelia; we're dying out here.

EMILIA1: Calm down Katherine. They don't want me for marriage. I'm no threat.

LADY CORDELIA: And you're fine! Lord Howard has been all eyes on you all today.

LADY KATHERINE: Really?

LORD HOWARD appears.

He's coming this way!

LORD HOWARD: My ladies

They all curtsey.

Lady Katherine I wonder if you would permit me to say how fragrant you are.

LADY KATHERINE: I couldn't possibly allow such boldness.

LORD HOWARD: But I pray that you will.

LADY KATHERINE: My lord I know not who you think I am but such a forward remark cannot go unpunished.

LORD HOWARD: I fear my sentence will be most lengthy. What do you have in mind?

LADY KATHERINE: Marriage?

LORD HOWARD: Perhaps a dance first?

LADY KATHERINE and LORD HOWARD exit.

LADY CORDELIA: Oh lord will I ever meet someone who will sweep me off my feet like that?

LORD COLLINS arrives. He spots CORDELIA over the following and they make eyes at each other.

EMILIA1: Oh come on don't you want gentle touch and kind glances and conversation? Don't you want a man who will see you for how brilliant your mind is and ask you how you wish to live your life instead of telling you how your life will be lived?

LADY CORDELIA: Sorry Emilia I'm not listening, who is that stone cold fox over there?

EMILIA1: *(Discreetly.)* That's Lord Collins.

EMILIA1 clears the way.

LORD COLLINS: To what do I owe the absolute pleasure?

LADY CORDELIA: Lady Cordelia my Lord. Are you terribly rich and powerful?

LORD COLLINS: Not in the slightest but I'd keep you in dresses and we'd tumble every day.

LADY CORDELIA: Dance with me fool before I change my mind.

He leads her away, she smiles over her shoulder at EMILIA1 as she goes. The dancers return but suddenly EMILIA1 sees her mother MARGARET JOHNSON across the floor from her. She is surprised by this and tries to get to her through the dancers. She can't reach her and her mother disappears. EMILIA1 drops to her knees.

EMILIA3: Only eight years since my father left me that I was to meet death again. My mother.

1587

The court dances are disbanded.

EMILIA1: Where is home now?

LORD HENRY CAREY approaches her.

LORD CAREY: My lady Emilia.

EMILIA1: Lord Henry Carey.

LORD CAREY: Would you give me the great pleasure of a dance?

EMILIA1: Would you permit me to decline?

LORD CAREY: That is your choice. Perhaps we could talk instead?

EMILIA1: Only if I can stay my tongue.

LORD CAREY: You would rather I talk without response from you?

EMILIA1: Sir I am weary of advances and my tongue would like a rest.

LORD CAREY: Do you have so many advances you feel I am unworthy of an audience?

EMILIA1: No sir. I am just weary. It isn't you. It is all of you. Must we continue these approaches until a match is made? Is it possible that perhaps a woman could choose never to match and instead live her life in pursuit of something greater?

LORD CAREY: What could be greater than love?

EMILIA1: Oh come now. How many of these marriages are the product of love? If you do seek love, and I know that I do, then seek it in poetry. Seek it in verse. In words written and spoken. Seek it in the pursuit of beauty. In art. For that, is the only place that will ever hold true love for me.

LORD CAREY: Then how about an old fool who looks not for marriage but for connection.

EMILIA1: Oh.

LORD CAREY: I know you Emilia Bassano. I've watched you for quite some time. You gently step round the edges of courtly life giving only the minimum of yourself so as to be noticed but not seen. I watch how you suffer the attentions of men your age who find your looks exciting but don't quite know what to do with you. I feel you don't yet know what to do with yourself.

EMILIA1: You 'feel' wrong.

LORD CAREY: Perhaps but if you were clear on how this world works you would maybe know more about where you wish to place yourself in it.

EMILIA1: What do you mean?

LORD CAREY: Maybe what you seek is security enough to continue to write and pursue your creative desires whilst also enjoying the careful passions of a man who has been in this game a long time and enjoys many privileges as a result. Those privileges can be shared. I could open some doors for you. I know The Countess of Pembroke well.

EMILIA1: Mary Sidney?

She high fives someone in the front row or box.

LORD CAREY: She is a great patron of the arts. Her property, Wilton House, has been described as 'Paradise for Poets' and should you wish I could arrange an introduction.

EMILIA1: Would you do that for me?

LORD CAREY: Well that depends. Will you meet me in my chambers in twenty minutes?

EMILIA1: I don't know.

LORD CAREY: *(Passing her a note.)* They are not far, which gives you ten minutes to decide. I cannot offer you marriage

Mistress Bassano but what I can offer you is worth much, much more.

He leaves. She stands taken aback.

EMILIA1: He's at least sixty years old! What confidence to approach me. And yet. He doesn't dismiss my desires like the others. Does he see me? If I do not go to him perhaps I will meet a man of my age to marry and bear children with. Someone I will serve as dutiful wife while he pursues his own wants. That would be the correct path for me. That would be the respectable and safe route. The one I have been trained for. My head sends me this way. But my heart. Oh my heart. Can I ignore its beating?

She takes a beat to decide then runs off in the direction LORD CAREY went.

EMILIA3: Suddenly I was no longer a court curiosity. I was currency. A mistress of Lord Henry Carey was afforded an apartment in Somerset House and forty pounds a year, that's one hundred and twenty thousand to you. But most importantly to me he provided only the best connections. He indulged in my need for poetry and I was able to mix with others who did too.

SCENE 3

Wilton House. Enter EMILIA1, she marvels at the hundreds of books. MARY SIDNEY enters and watches EMILIA1 until she is noticed.

EMILIA1: My lady, Countess of Pembroke, I am humbled to have been granted an audience. My Lord Carey insisted I stay only a short while so as not to over step my place but I had hoped you would read my work for to have your opinion on it would do me so much pleasure.

MARY SIDNEY: Oh god don't grovel. I've read your work.
Henry sent it to me. You write with grace and confidence.

EMILIA1: Thank you!

MARY SIDNEY: You're not bad. As you probably know,
because those bitches in the court keep fake whispering
about it, I'm working on some Psalms my late brother did
not complete and I hope to publish them when I'm done.
Is this something you would also strive for?

EMILIA1: Well of course I can hope but surely the ones who
would publish would not permit it.

MARY SIDNEY: The men you mean?

EMILIA1: I do.

MARY SIDNEY: And yet Henry did tell me that you care little
for what men think.

EMILIA1: I don't. I mean. I do. But I've never considered it a
possibility that my words would ever be good enough to
be committed to print.

MARY SIDNEY: That is because you were not brought up as
they were with words of encouragement and the blithe
acceptance that you would be destined for great things.
Do not underestimate what power that has. No matter
what obstacles this system holds around us we must
always strive to find ways to get whatever it is we so
desperately desire. I desire my poems be published. And
I will see that they are. You, Emilia Bassano, will one day
do the same.

EMILIA1: But how?

MARY SIDNEY: Well I don't know but if you keep writing you'll
conspire of an answer. And in the meantime perhaps you

will come and sit with me a while. I want to find out what it is Henry is so enthusiastic about.

LADY MARGARET CLIFFORD has entered in the previous and quickly interrupts.

LADY MARGARET: Now now Mary let's not prey on a young lady's naivete.

MARY SIDNEY: Oh god who let you in?

LADY MARGARET: What a pleasure to see you too. I came as soon as I heard you had Mistress Bassano visiting as I had hoped to speak to her about a position but I see you were already attempting to get her into one ahead of me.

MARY SIDNEY: You really are the most dreadful box blocker Margaret. I found her first. She's much too exotic for you.

LADY MARGARET: How do you feel about that description Emilia? Are you an exotic curiosity?

MARY SIDNEY: *(Interrupts.)* Oh come now you know full well I wished only to encourage her pursuit of poetry.

LADY MARGARET: Emilia, my name is Lady Margaret Clifford and I have been admiring you from afar. I come with an offer of employment. My daughter Anne will be ready for a personal tutor soon and I have heard great things about your intellect. Perhaps you would consider joining me in creating another young lady with hopes beyond being considered a mere object of desire.

MARY SIDNEY: Oh Lord how dreary. Emilia darling for heavensake say no. You are destined for greater things than servitude. This is a dead end. Say no.

EMILIA1: I am most flattered at the offer. Will you permit me to think on it? I'm suddenly feeling a little conflicted.

LADY MARGARET: You don't have to answer now. Remember me if you need. Anything.

EMILIA3 speaks to the rest of the company suddenly.

EMILIA3: This moment.

LADY MARGARET: But Emilia beware the ones who appear as ally but play to the same tune as the enemy.

EMILIA3: That.

MARY SIDNEY: What was that supposed to mean?

LADY MARGARET starts to walk off.

LADY MARGARET: It means it's time for me to leave.

MARY SIDNEY: Dear god go already! Guards! Take her away.

LADY MARGARET: You don't have guards for heavens sake. I'm going. Emilia. The offer is always there.

LADY MARGARET leaves as WILLIAM SHAKESPEARE enters – he isn't noticed by MARY or EMILIA1 and stays back and watches over the following.

MARY SIDNEY: You will do well to stay well away from her. It's common knowledge her husband is so bored of her he has a different mistress every week.

EMILIA1: And why should that keep me from Lady Margaret?

MARY SIDNEY: Her reputation is in pieces dear. You must be very careful who you associate with. You're on a very fine line as it is. You're not like the other girls, you do know that don't you? Henry can only protect you so far. Now, I'm bored. Play the game well Emilia and you will succeed. And when I say 'well' I mean 'safely'...for all our sakes.

SHAKESPEARE hovers on the edge waiting for MARY but watching EMILIA1.

I have to go, I have another engagement. Do you know Will Shakespeare?

EMILIA1: I don't.

MARY SIDNEY: Will this is Emilia Bassano but she's not your type.

Before he can approach EMILIA1 or even speak he has been taken by the hand and lead out. He smiles at EMILIA1 as he goes.

(Shouting as she leaves.) Keep writing Emilia! Even if no one wants to read it. Isn't that right Will?

They're gone. EMILIA1 is left in their wake.

SCENE 4

EMILIA1 goes to work on her own. MUSIC. She writes and writes. Paper and poems fly around her.

LORD CAREY approaches.

LORD CAREY: My love, I have twenty minutes.

EMILIA1: Oh!

LORD CAREY: I have to return to court.

EMILIA1: How romantic.

LORD CAREY: Stop teasing. Nineteen minutes. I'll lose my window of opportunity.

EMILIA1: Nineteen minutes is generous for your purposes.

LORD CAREY: Watch it.

EMILIA1: Please.

LORD CAREY: What is it?

EMILIA3 halts action

EMILIA3: Safe. Safely. Carefully. Quietly. Calmly. We must abide. We must toe the rope. We mustn't show our teeth. Be careful. Here it comes.

EMILIA1: My lord I've been trying to find words that will not condemn me to a life of poverty. But there is no easy way to give you the plain truth.

LORD CAREY: *(Smiling.)* What wickedness have you performed now?

EMILIA1: My love I carry your child.

LORD CAREY immediately lets go of her. A long pause as she waits breathless for his response.

Please speak.

LORD CAREY: You won't be left wanting.

EMILIA1: Henry.

LORD CAREY: I'll arrange everything for you.

EMILIA1: Arrange what?

LORD CAREY: We'll speak anon.

He strides away. She tries to grab him but he slips her grasp.

EMILIA1: Please!

She is left alone. Except for the other two EMILIAs.

My heart. From the very moment I uttered the words I felt him begin to untie the knots. Can I run now? Where to?

And what of my child? I couldn't run so much as a bear in a pit could.

She exits. LORD CAREY enters with ALPHONSO LANIER – he is dressed flamboyantly and extravagantly for a court musician. He possesses a descant recorder.

ALPHONSO : I cannot love her. She is my cousin. And besides it is a poor match for me. My father expected better.

LORD CAREY: Your father had little to no expectation for you and this match is above anything you could have ever hoped to have achieved.

ALPHONSO: She is not to my taste.

EMILIA1 re-enters.

LORD CAREY: Your tastes need refinement.

ALPHONSO: She is soiled goods.

LORD CAREY: *(Furious.)* Proud, scornful boy, unworthy of this good gift! Check thy contempt! What you have before you is a flower of such sweetness and beauty. A viper of such strength and cunning. A temptress who will beguile the very clothes off your back. Do not underestimate this jewel.

EMILIA1: Can the jewel speak?

LORD CAREY: Emilia this is the best way.

EMILIA1: It is so far from the best it is back round to the worst. Alphonso? ALPHONSO? What are you doing Henry?

ALPHONSO: Thank you!

EMILIA1: Do you not want me to be happy?

LORD CAREY takes her to one side.

LORD CAREY: This is the perfect solution. He won't want of you and you have no need to give to him. We can continue our meetings but for colour you will appear virtuous.

EMILIA1: With Alphonso?!

LORD CAREY: I know, I know but think. He won't care. Look at him.

They both look over at Alphonso who is preening himself in a mirror.

He cares more for himself than for any woman.

EMILIA1: It's not women I'll be competing with that's for sure.

LORD CAREY: You won't need to compete at all.

EMILIA1: I cannot marry someone I do not love.

LORD CAREY: You can. And you must.

EMILIA1: And you won't abandon me?

LORD CAREY: I won't.

EMILIA1: What have you offered him?

LORD CAREY: My care. You will be provided for.

EMILIA1: I only do this for you.

LORD CAREY: And I for you. Lanier?

ALPHONSO comes over.

It is agreed.

ALPHONSO: Not by me!

LORD CAREY: Let me be very clear. If you are not obedient then I will throw you from my care and worse you will suffer both my revenge and hate which I will set loose on

you in the name of justice. Without any chance of pity.
Speak your answer now.

ALPHONSO: Well when you put it like that. How can a man
refuse?

LORD CAREY: Good answer. Come. We'll lay out our terms.

*He takes ALPHONSO away without a backward glance at EMILIA1.
She stands in shock as EMILIA2 and EMILIA3 speak. Over the
following EMILIA1 is dressed in her wedding dress by handmaids.*

EMILIA3: Was I a trawl of fish or stack of hay? Was I meat?
What else was there for me now? His hook in me digs
deeper, burrows further into my flesh so that it can assert
it's ownership over my body. He has covered all inches
of me. While he discusses what to do with my future. His
seed is busy making home of my now. What were these
feelings growing in me? The flutterings of a tiny creature
making himself known or was it something else? It was a
strange feeling indeed. A growing sense of unease.

EMILIA2: A flickering flame. Heat.

EMILIA3: I felt heat. Of something starting. Something that
has lain quiet and still for some time. Held down. Buried.
And this unspeakable action by my lord has awakened
it somehow. I knew that I would marry that man but no
longer for my love.

EMILIA2: I did it for my child.

EMILIA3: For me? I would begin to fan this flame so as to see
how bright it would burn.

SCENE 5

Music. The Wedding Of ALPHONSO LANIER *and* EMILIA BASSANO. *A motif that shows the transfer over from* LORD CAREY *to* ALPHONSO. *The couple are married. The kiss is an awkward peck. They pull away from each other as soon as it's done.* ALPHONSO *goes to his friends.* EMILIA *immediately bumps into someone. It's* SHAKESPEARE.

EMILIA1: I'm so sorry!

SHAKESPEARE: The fault was mine. My lady...

EMILIA1: Emilia Bassano...sorry; Lanier. It's Lanier now.

SHAKESPEARE: Congratulations.

EMILIA1: We met once did we not? Lady Mary Sidney's home.

SHAKESPEARE: Of course! The dark lady I never got the chance to speak with. My name is William Shakespeare. But you can call me Will. If you like, you don't have to.

A brief moment that they share.

Your husband approaches.

He leaves. EMILIA *is disappointed and turns to* ALPHONSO *who approaches merrily.*

ALPHONSO: I'm going to go and celebrate our marriage my dear.

EMILIA1: Where?

ALPHONSO: With my friends.

A group of rowdy men cheer and raise glasses.

EMILIA1: I mean tradition does dictate that a man must spend the first night with his wife....but...

ALPHONSO: Oh no no no. Fret not! It's far more fashionable for the groom to go and toast the beauty of his wife

with friends. I'll return anon and we can complete our...
business then.

He leaves.

EMILIA1: I can hardly wait.

He's gone.

What am I to do now? Go to my Lord Carey? Chase
my new husband? I know not. No. I *care* not. I am done
dancing towards them. They will have to dance to me.

She is about to sweep off when she bumps into SHAKESPEARE.

Oh!

SHAKESPEARE: I didn't mean to startle you my lady. I was
simply returning to pay you my many congratulations.

EMILIA1: You already did.

SHAKESPEARE: Sorry?

EMILIA1: Before. You have already congratulated me.

SHAKESPEARE: Well then I do it again. Congratulations.

EMILIA1: That's a bit weird isn't it?

SHAKESPEARE: Pardon?

EMILIA1: If you wanted to say something else just say it I
cannot be more done with the verbal dances we have to
do all the time.

SHAKESPEARE: Oh I see.

EMILIA1: Now what?

SHAKESPEARE: I'm sorry I just/

EMILIA1: I'm going.

SHAKESPEARE: No please! When we met the first time I didn't
   have a chance to properly introduce myself but I was
   taken by your charm.

EMILIA1: You liked my face you mean.

SHAKESPEARE: Yes

EMILIA1: My skin.

SHAKESPEARE: Yes.

EMILIA1: You find me intriguing perhaps? You find me a
   'breath of fresh air'. You find me exciting maybe. You
   want to give me a try. You want to see whether things are
   different with me. You want to even perhaps rescue me.
   Perhaps you want to sweep me off and coddle me. Protect
   me. Perhaps you want to sympathise with me. Pity me. Be
   my champion. Encourage me. Step into the heroes shoes
   and alter my fate. Is that it? Because I've heard all of this
   before. A thousand times from all the men who skulk past
   and sniff at me like dogs. I don't care who you are but you
   will not be able to say or give me anything I have not had
   before. And besides, I'm married now. You should find
   someone better suited to your attentions.

   She goes to leave.

SHAKESPEARE: You're so angry. Why? You're like a trapped
   wasp.

EMILIA1: Alright. We're doing this are we?

SHAKESPEARE: Doing what?

EMILIA1: You know what. Fine. Let's do it. If I am a wasp, best
   beware my sting.

SHAKESPEARE: If you sting me I'll pluck it out.

EMILIA1: Ay if you can find it.

SHAKESPEARE: Who doesn't know where a wasp keeps his sting? It's in his tail!

EMILIA1: In his tongue.

SHAKESPEARE: Who's tongue?

EMILIA1: Your tongue if you don't leave me be.

SHAKESPEARE: Is this...I mean...are we? I don't know what this is.

EMILIA1: I do know of you, you know. How can I not? I hear you are a poet.

SHAKESPEARE: I am.

EMILIA1: Me too.

SHAKESPEARE: You write?

EMILIA1: I do.

They circle each other. They're wooing each other.

SHAKESPEARE: How oft, when thou, my music, music play'st,
Upon that blessed wood whose motion sounds
With thy sweet fingers, when thou gently sway'st
The wiry concord that mine ear confounds,
Do I envy those jacks that nimble leap
To kiss the tender inward of thy hand,
Whilst my poor lips, which should that harvest reap
At the wood's boldness by thee blushing stand!
To be so tickled, they would change their state
And situation with those dancing chips,
O'er whom thy fingers walk with gentle gait,
Making dead wood more blest than living lips.
Since saucy jacks so happy are in this,
Give them thy fingers, me thy lips to kiss.

She seems like she is going to kiss him then turns away at the last moment leaving Shakespeare frustrated. At some point over the following he gives her a rose.

EMILIA1: How I would make him fawn, and beg, and seek,
    And wait the season, and observe the time,
    And spend his prodigal wits in bootless rhymes,
    And shape his service wholly to my hests,
    And make him proud to make me proud that jests!
    So pertaunt like would I o'ersway his state
    That he should be my fool, and I his fate.

She gives the rose to someone in the audience. Shakespeare reacts angrily. Over the following EMILIA1 reacts to his insults.

SHAKESPEARE: My mistress' eyes are nothing like the sun;
    Coral is far more red than her lips' red:
    If snow be white, why then her breasts are dun;
    If hairs be wires, black wires grow on her head.

EMILIA1: That's racist!

SHAKESPEARE: I have seen roses damask'd, red and white,
    But no such roses see I in her cheeks;
    And in some perfumes is there more delight
    Than in the breath that from my mistress reeks.
    I love to hear her speak, yet well I know
    That music hath a far more pleasing sound:
    I grant I never saw a goddess go;
    My mistress, when she walks, treads on the ground.
    And yet, by heaven, I think my love as rare
    As any she belied with false compare

EMILIA3: I carried Henry's child but it was Will's heart that I
    came to cherish.

EMILIA1: Come, gentle night, come, loving, black-brow'd
   night,
   Give me my Will, and, when I shall die,
   Take him and cut him out in little stars,
   And he will make the face of heaven so fine
   That all the world will be in love with night,
   And pay no worship to the garish sun.

   Suddenly EMILIA1 cries out.

   Stop!

   She grabs her belly and looks up at SHAKESPEARE in fear.

SHAKESPEARE: Oh shit. I'll get help! Midwife!

   He runs off.

SCENE 6

1592

The MIDWIFE runs on and EMILIA roar in pain.

MIDWIFE: Here! Now you listen to me. You push when I say.
   You stop when I say. Anything in between? You do what I
   say. You understand?

EMILIA1: Yes. But I want to push. Can I push?

MIDWIFE: Hold up!

   She looks under EMILIA1's skirts.

   No, no, no , no, YES PUSH!

   *The birth is a bustling affair with lots of calm reassurances from the
   MIDWIFE and yelling from EMILIA1. Choral voices. EMILIA1 cradles
   her new son. ALPHONSO bursts in.*

29

ALPHONSO: I came as soon as I could! Is it safe to view my child?

MIDWIFE: It is.

ALPHONSO: It's just I'm no good around blood and gore.

MIDWIFE: You just missed that.

ALPHONSO: Small mercies. Do I have a son?

MIDWIFE: I'll let your wife tell you that.

ALPHONSO approaches.

EMILIA1: I'll call him Henry.

ALPHONSO: Really?

EMILIA1: Let's make sure we're never forgotten by him.

ALPHONSO: Clever woman.

He kisses her on the head.

He's got your eyes. They're very lovely. And his cheeks are/

EMILIA1: You're allowed to go now.

ALPHONSO: Oh thank god. Good bye my love. I'm off to fight in a war.

EMILIA1: Do whatever you need to do. I am content. Try not to spend all of our money.

ALPHONSO: That would be good! Oh! And well done for not dying. That would have been a massive drag.

The baby cries and so ALPHONSO exits.

EMILIA1: Shush little one. Are you so sad that you have come? This great stage of fools? It won't be so bad. It won't be so bad.

SCENE 7

We see a brief moment of SHAKESPEARE and EMILIA1 as lovers which is interrupted by HENRY CAREY before he speaks. Then over the following scene we see various moments occur including SHAKESPEARE watching from a small distance away. EMILIA1 tries to nurse her child but the MIDWIFE is constantly taking him from her. She is also desperately trying to write. She is also torn by her love of SHAKESPEARE and he distracts her from her mothering AND her work. She oscillates between him and LORD CAREY. The two of them demanding her attention one after the other.

LORD CAREY: You do know that rumours are rife about you?

EMILIA1: You don't believe any of them do you?

LORD CAREY: Of course I don't.

EMILIA1: Good. Can you stay?

LORD CAREY: No. I'm called to court. We are assembling a company of actors – we're naming it after me; the Lord Chamberlain's Men! Young Will Shakespeare is making a real name for himself. You wouldn't want to ruin that for him would you?

She jumps back into the moment with SHAKESPEARE.

EMILIA1: I dare not be the reason your play is late. What have you called it?

SHAKESPEARE: I know not.

EMILIA1: Then I shall name it. My Love. Your Labour. Your lost son.

SHAKESPEARE: Catchy.

EMILIA1: Love. Labour and Loss.

SHAKESPEARE: You don't even know what it's about yet.

EMILIA1: I can guess. Mistaken identity, notes passed, silly boys and women who could do better?

SHAKESPEARE: Well now you mention it.

EMILIA1: Make sure there is resistance from the women. I want there to be one who does not wish to marry. Who is being forced to marry. Let me be able to relate to someone. Someone who has not been given what she deserves.

SHAKESPEARE: Why wait to be given? Why not take?

EMILIA1: You try taking when you are as I am. You try just taking. You can speak as you do because of who you are. What you are. You try stepping in my shoes.

SHAKESPEARE: You have your own talents my love. If you strive you too can achieve the same as I.

She jumps into a moment with LORD CAREY

LORD CAREY: He has talent. Talent doesn't need distraction.

EMILIA1: What if it is I that is getting distracted?

LORD CAREY: From what?

EMILIA1: My work.

LORD CAREY: Well alright but yours is more of a hobby isn't it?

EMILIA1: Would you consider something of mine for your men? I could write a play.

LORD CAREY begins laughing hard.

LORD CAREY: Oh you are glorious. I must go. Just be careful. We need him.

He leaves. EMILIA turns back to SHAKESPEARE.

SHAKESPEARE: What did you think he was going to say?

EMILIA1: *(Furious.)* Am I not permitted to have what you have?

SHAKESPEARE: Be careful Emilia. Anger will not serve you well.

EMILIA1: Anger serves me just fine! Anger will fuel me. Anger will turn hope into action. Do not take my anger from me.

SHAKESPEARE: You cannot be angry with me?

EMILIA1: Why not?

SHAKESPEARE: Have I not worked hard? And are you not happy for me?

EMILIA1: How bitter a thing it is to look into happiness through another's eyes.

SHAKESPEARE: That's very cruel.

EMILIA1: If you think I'm cruel to speak this truth then you will think me murderous if all my truth were known.

SHAKESPEARE: You're shaking. What's wrong you?

EMILIA1: It feels like morning. I'm waking up.

SHAKESPEARE: Your words! This passion! Yes. Love's, Labour's, Lost. I can write this. I will write this tonight. And my heart, it will be in tribute to you. Let me help your words find a stage. Let me pour you into my work and immortalise your soul.

He grabs her and kisses her then turns to grab his quill and parchment and leaves in a hurry. Over the following EMILIA1 is strapped into a pregnancy bump.

EMILIA1: Is this what it feels like now? Is this it? Have I reached my summit? Should I now rest here and watch the heights that can be reached on other mountains by them? Looking up through the clouds. Searching and straining to watch them triumphantly conquer higher, more beautiful, more bountiful mountains that are not mine to climb? Is this it?

LADY CORDELIA enters

LADY CORDELIA: Emilia! Have you heard the news? Your Lord is dead!

EMILIA1: Alphonso?

LADY CORDELIA: Lord Carey.

EMILIA1: No!

LADY CORDELIA: Last night.

EMILIA1: Can I see him?

LADY CORDELIA: His wife is in attendance.

LADY CORDELIA exits. EMILIA1 is rocked by this news. Everyone has eyes on her. She stands and composes herself.

EMILIA3: There was never any love without pain. My belly was full and round again. Over the crest of a wave I went. Again and again and again.

EMILIA1 howls in labour and gives birth. A repeat of her previous birth but quicker.

SCENE 8

EMILIA1: *(To her new baby.)* Oh the life you could have had if you had not been born as I. Little eyes stay closed so you don't see the fate you are headed towards. Together. We'll do all this together.

ALPHONSO arrives.

ALPHONSO: Well what immaculate conception could this be? Did I pop back from battle nine months ago? A son?

EMILIA1: A daughter. Odilya.

ALPHONSO: Well she is of no interest to me. Is Henry prospering?

EMILIA1: He is well. I assume. I get letters from school. I barely see him. You hear about Lord Carey.

ALPHONSO: I did.

EMILIA1: I trust you are being careful with our funds.

ALPHONSO: Must you ask? I trust you are being discreet?

EMILIA1: As ever.

ALPHONSO: Clever woman.

SHAKESPEARE has been watching and waits for ALPHONSO to leave before he approaches with a Moses basket. EMILIA1 puts the baby in his arms.

SHAKESPEARE: Is she...?

EMILIA1: Yes.

SHAKESPEARE: You know that I cannot...

EMILIA1: I know. Your play? Is it open?

SHAKESPEARE gently returns the baby to EMILIA1

SHAKESPEARE: Yes. Much Ado About Nothing. They love it. In fact. I'm due at the theatre now.

EMILIA1 turns to get her notepad, while she does SHAKESPEARE leaves.

EMILIA1: I've written something new also. In the bleary moments between night feeds. It's all I can do but I think it might be good. I know you're busy and probably have plenty of your own work to be doing but will you read it? Tell me what you think.

She turns and sees he's gone.

EMILIA3: Are you ready?

EMILIA2: Yes.

Over the following EMILIA1 has placed the baby in it's Moses basket and takes the opportunity to write. EMILIA3 approaches the crib and when it feels right takes the opportunity to lift the baby and cuddle her then finally replace her.

EMILIA3: Some women will say that when they give birth they lose something of themselves to their child. That somehow this tiny parasite that has grown within them has managed to sneak something out of her and will now keep it as their own forever. They see this as the stolen sleep and time. They see this in the changes to their body or the pains they will forever have. They see this in the way their lives before will never now return to them as they will have to pour all their energy into their child so that they can instead be the one that thrives. Not many mothers will begrudge this but some will. I did not begrudge this. But I did feel a loss. Yet it was worth it; I thought that I could bring up a daughter who was perhaps stronger than me. Perhaps would benefit from a changing landscape. Have more chances than I did. And I knew that I would fight for her. So even though I felt the loss I also saw the gain. And for me, Odilya, was hope.

Everyone watches EMILIA1 as she speaks to her daughter. The other EMILIA's join her.

EMILIA1: Hello sweet girl.

EMILIA2: Will you wake?

EMILIA1: Let's go out for a walk.

EMILIA3: Odilya?

EMILIA2: Will you?

EMILIA1 gently shakes her then after another moment she rips at the baby's clothing.

EMILIA1: Odilya?

EMILIA2: Wake up.

She holds her baby to her face and tries to feel her breath.

EMILIA3: Breath.

EMILIA2: Breath for me.

EMILIA1: Please. No no no no no.

She is on her knees holding her baby to her. The baby is taken from her. EMILIA2 and EMILIA3 have joined her.

EMILIA3: You've done so well.

They swap places. EMILIA1 is helped off by EMILIA3 and the ensemble. EMILIA2 is left alone in her grief.

SCENE 9

SHAKESPEARE enters.

SHAKESPEARE: I heard. Are you alright?

EMILIA2: No.

SHAKESPEARE: What can I do?

EMILIA2: Nothing.

SHAKESPEARE: Nothing will come of nothing.

EMILIA2: I cannot heave my heart into my mouth. There are no words for what I am feeling.

SHAKESPEARE: I know my love.

EMILIA2: Do you?

SHAKESPEARE: You know I do.

EMILIA2: And yet you find them. Again and again. The pain and anguish of your own losses written large upon the stage. Does it help? I think it must. If only my own grief could be dissipated as such. But it can't. Can it? And it is because of this that grief is not my only pain. It is my whole existence in your shadow. It is women born to a status that dooms us to your ill will. That there be women that do abuse their husbands I am of no doubt but the balance is grossly tipped in your favour. That we must assume that everything we do is to be dismissed. That all talent and interest, all passion and sense is just a quirk of our sex that can be indulged but never validated. That we must instead sit quietly and patiently watch as you enjoy the fruits of your labours. Imagine it so for you. Then see how my own desires languish in the dark. And still your sex think we are less? That we have less, to be able to survive? That somehow perhaps we feel less? Well I would that you use your privileged position in that wooden O of words to let husbands know, their wives have sense like them. They see and smell and have their palates, both for sweet and sour, as husbands have. What is it that they do when they change us for others? Is it sport? I think it is. And does affection breed it? I think it does. Is it frailty, that thus errs? It is so too. And have not we affections. Desires for sport, and frailty, as men have? Then let them use us well; else let them know, the ills we do, their ills instruct us so. Get out.

SHAKESPEARE: Emilia you are full of grief. Stop.

EMILIA2: Get out!

SHAKESPEARE: I will return when you are at peace.

EMILIA2: I will never be at peace as long as I have no voice!

SHAKESPEARE leaves.

I will not stop. I will not rest until I find words for my Odilya. And for all my daughters I will never know.

SCENE 10

LADY KATHERINE arrives.

EMILIA2: Will you help me? I need money to publish my poetry. I can change things. For us all. I know it.

LADY KATHERINE: Listen to me Emilia; you have lost Lord Carey and your yearly stipend, your husband is an idiot who spends more money than he has, you have no other lovers to pay for you and soon you will be driven to the streets. You are throwing away years of hard work and your father and mother, if they were with you now, would be urging you the same as me. This battle is not yours to fight.

EMILIA2: Then whose is it?

LADY KATHERINE: Not yours. You speak as if you do not live a life of privilege when you do. You are fine. You can still be fine. Why would you want to throw this away?

EMILIA2: I know I can still be fine and I know my privilege, I am reminded of it every day. Every time I am looked upon with surprised eyes. When I'm lusted over. When I am questioned as to whether I should be in court or did I get lost on my way up from downstairs. I doubt you've ever suffered the same.

LADY KATHERINE: It's hardly a suffering.

EMILIA2: You don't get to say that unless you've experienced it. Have you not heard the way the men in court discuss those coming here to seek a home? To seek work? To seek peace and solace? Have you not noticed how they are no longer interested in what skills people bring but whether they 'belong' here or not? Have you not felt a change? These families, coming here, they are like mine. I'm no longer a curiosity. I'm something else now. I can't sit by and do nothing.

LADY KATHERINE: Find the path you were trained for and rejoin it. Be sensible Emilia.

EMILIA2: 'Sensible' has never changed anything Katherine.

LADY KATHERINE: Then I must go.

She leaves.

SCENE 11

As EMILIA2 speaks she paces. She walks the stage but eventually joins the groundlings. Stalking everywhere. She has come to the Globe to see SHAKESPEARE'S latest play OTHELLO and the actors prepare themselves on stage.

EMILIA2: I must walk the shore of the river on Bankside. I must breathe in the filth and smoke and smells of the water that brought us here. I must surround myself with the rest of us. I find myself at the Globe. It's busier here than before. There's a buzz. A new play is on. I go into the yard amongst people like me, people not like me, people. I go into the yard and for a moment I let myself look at the stage as if expecting to see my own work there. For we are told this. That the art is for escape and we should simply transpose our own image upon it. Use

40

our imaginations. That should be enough shouldn't it?
But there is only so much work our imaginations can do.
When the image we see is so far from our truth we cannot
see a place for us. Is there no room at all? We do not ask
for them to step aside and go without we merely ask them
to let us join. Surely there is enough to go around.

*Suddenly she sees SHAKESPEARE who walks through the dress circle
to the box. He is enjoying his fame.*

Will?

SHAKESPEARE: Ay? Autographs at stage door thank you.

EMILIA2: Do you ignore me now?

SHAKESPEARE: You were the one who told me to go.

EMILIA2: But now I see you have much to do.

SHAKESPEARE: It's a busy time. The Globe needs plays. I'm
writing more than I ever have. My latest is a triumph.
Othello. I play Iago. It is about a Moor. It's right up your
street.

EMILIA2: I'm happy for you.

SHAKESPEARE: Are you?

EMILIA2: I'm happy you've found your voice so strongly.
Perhaps it is because I am no longer your muse?

SHAKESPEARE: You never were.

EMILIA2: What?

SHAKESPEARE: You were my lover but I had other muses. This
is all rather public isn't it? So sorry! Excuse me

*He exits to come down. EMILIA2 is made to wait. SHAKESPEARE
arrives on stage.*

Look, you were my sparring partner. You challenged me of course. But I did not need you for my work.

EMILIA2: And yet you were happy to use my words.

SHAKESPEARE: They aren't yours. No one owns words spoken. No one owns what they've said. What absurdity. After all you can speak with passion and eloquence but when you come to put it onto a page it is a harder craft than you may imagine. I have the talent to recognise phrases or speeches that can be used and I craft them into my scripts to tell the story I wish them to tell. That is where the skill lies. Not in simply speaking. It means nothing until it is on a page.

EMILIA2: Do not assume to teach me my craft. I am not a schoolgirl staring up at you in adoration. You are explaining what I already know. Why is it only men do this? You speak as if I cannot already write.

SHAKESPEARE: You can.

EMILIA2: And yet I should not have recognition for it? Should not publish? Not be commissioned as you?

SHAKESPEARE: No.

EMILIA2: Why not?

SHAKESPEARE: ...

EMILIA2: Will? Why can I not do as you do?

SHAKESPEARE: ...

EMILIA2: You know why. Say it.

A musical flourish.

SHAKESPEARE: Good luck Emilia. Act 4 is beginning I need to go.

EMILIA2: My words! You've used my words and stories in so
many of your plays and yet only your name is known.

SHAKESPEARE: *(Angry.)* Now you listen to me. Those plays are
MY work. I toiled over them. I wrote them. Me. There is
a big difference between having an idea to write and being
the one who actually does it.

EMILIA2: But I do write!

SHAKESPEARE: I will not be held at fault for the rules of our
time.

EMILIA2: And yet you prosper from them.

SHAKESPEARE: What would you have me do? Down tools?
Refuse to write unless women are also given the same
freedoms?

EMILIA2: Yes!

SHAKESPEARE: Well I won't. And neither would you if you
were I.

Some voices call for him from elsewhere.

BOB. Will!

DAVE: We've got your beer.

SHAKESPEARE: Just a sparkling water for me...need to protect
my voice...!

BOB: It's starting!

SHAKESPEARE: Good day Emilia. How about you try enjoying
the show instead of taking offence at any similarities
to your words within it try being flattered. Many other
women would die for the chance.

*He leaves. BOB and DAVE who he's joining cheer and laugh at him.
By now EMILIA2 is on the floor with the Groundlings. Act 4 Scene*

2 of Othello is playing out. The Willow Song is shared between DESDEMONA and EMILIA. Whilst this happens SHAKESPEARE joins his friends in one box and EMILIA2 makes her way up to a box on the opposite side. The scene starts.

DESDEMONA: I have heard it said so. – O these men, these men! Dost thou in conscience think – tell me Emilia.

EMILIA3: She had my name.

EMILIA2: She has my name.

DESDEMONA: That there be women do abuse their husbands in such gross kind?

A musical note.

EMILIA3: There. This. Here.

DESDEMONA: Wouldst thou do such a deed for all the world?

EMILIA: Why, would not you?

DESDEMONA: No by this heavenly light!

EMILIA: Nor I neither by this heavenly light : I might do't as well i the dark.

EMILIA2: Ha! I like her.

DESDEMONA: Wouldst thou do such a deed for all the world?

EMILIA: The world is a huge thing; tis a great price for a small vice.

DESDEMONA: In troth, I think thou wouldst not.

EMILIA: In troth, I think I should, and undo't when I had done. Marry, I would not do such a thing for a joint-ring, nor for measures of lawn, nor for gowns, petticoats, nor caps, no any petty exhibition; but for the whle world – why who would not make her husband a cuckold, to make him a monarch? I should venture purgatory for 't.

EMILIA2: She speaks like I would. She seems like me. He's even used my name the bastard. Is he laughing at me? For this is not flattery. She speaks sense but they will not see it so. He is laughing at me. He says with this; look what I do that you cannot. And he expects my silence.

DESDEMONA: Beshrew me, if I would do such a wrong for the whole world.

EMILIA: Why the wrong is but a wrong i' the world; and having the world for your labour, 't is a wrong in your own world, and you might quickly make it right.

DESDEMONA: I do not think there is any such woman.

EMILIA: Yes a dozen; and as many to the vantage as would store the world they played for. But I do think, it is their husbands' faults, if wives do fall.

EMILIA2: Did I not say this to him on the pillow one night? I remember this. I did! I was furious with Alphonso! Oh these are mine! These are mine!

EMILIA: Say, that they slack their duties, and pour our treasures into foreign laps. Or else break out in peevish jealousies, Throwing restraint upon us; or say, they strike us, Or scant our former having in despite: Why we have galls; and, though we have some grace,

A musical note.

EMILIA3: Now!

EMILIA2 runs on stage.

EMILIA2 AND EMILIA: Yet have we some revenge.

The person playing EMILIA stops in shock and looks down towards EMILIA2 who continues the speech while battling her way through the Groundlings and to the stage.

EMILIA2: Let husbands know, their wives have sense like them: they see and smell, And have their palates, both for sweet and sour. As husbands have. What is it that they do, when they change us for others? Is it sport? I think , it is. And doth affection breed it? I think it doth.

DESDEMONA: There's a woman on the stage!

Over the following the attendees of the performance of Othello react in outrage and amazement. No one at first knows what to do but eventually they make it to stage to get rid of her.

Its't frailty, that thus errs? It is so too. And have not we affections, desires for sport and frailty, as men have? Then let them use us well; else let them know, the ills we do, their ills instruct us so.

By now she is centre stage addressing the crowd. She is furious and powerful. A couple of officials try to grab her and drag her off but she pulls away from them and beats her feet chanting:

The ills we do, their ills instruct us so!

This becomes a chant. Drums. She is watched but not joined. It feels like she is winning but then finally she is over come by people trying to stop her and she is dragged from the stage still shouting.

BOB: Music!

EMILIA2: The ills we do, their ills instruct us so!

BOB: Curtain!

END OF ACT 1

ACT 2

1603. The Bankside washer women enter. They sing 'Fare Thew Well Old Joe Clark' whilst they work.

Fare thee well old Joe Clark
Fare thee well I'm gone
Fare thee well old Joe Clark
And bring back Betsy brown

When I was a little girl
I used to play with boys
But now I am a bigger girl
I only play with 'toys'

Chorus repeat

When I was a little girl
I used to want a knife
And now I am a bigger girl
I only want a wife

Fare thee well old Joe Clark
Fare thee well I'm gone
Fare thee well old Joe Clark
And hello Betsy brown

EMILIA2: Bankside. Walked the stretch with the filth, the washer women and the hawkers. Unaccompanied and probably looked lost. No one bothered me. They looked but no one asked me who I was. Why I was here. What I was doing. They have no care for me. Why should they? I looked at the tide line and I found treasure in the filth. It had travelled up the beach and been abandoned there on the ebb. Amongst the clay pipes and food and bones and broken pots I found a seed pod. Not from here. Why had it washed up here? And what would now become of it? It had been in the water long enough to attract barnacles but now it had reached shore it found a land unforgiving. It was not welcome. What use was it here? What I should have done was thrown it back to the river and hope it finds it's way home. Or even perhaps left it to fester on the beach. That's what I should have done. But I just wanted to hold it. I just needed to hold onto something

EMILIA3: I was looking at the water for long enough for it to draw me closer. Like the lapping of the waves were pulling me.

EMILIA1: I must have started to wade in. I must have looked like I was trying to swim.

JUDITH: Oi Lady! You lost?

EVE: She mad?

JUDITH: She might be.

EVE: What is she doing?

JUDITH: We've got a live one.

EMILIA3: I must have looked like I was sinking. Because the voices got closer and then they, then they, then....

EVE: Jesus christ almighty Jude what is she doing?

JUDITH: Quick! Help me grab her!

EMILIA3: Here's another of those moments. Another of those times.

A note sounds.

They are joined by EVE, MARY *and* FLORA *and between the five of them, and all shouting at each other and* EMILIA2 *they grab and carry her out of the river and to safety.*

HESTER: Not on my watch lady.

MARY : Is she breathing?

They wait to see if she's ok and EMILIA2 *opens her eyes.*

FLORA: Hello missus. Fancied a swim?

EMILIA2: What happened?

HESTER: You got yourself into trouble in the river there.

MARY: We hoiked you out.

EMILIA2: The seed pod.

JUDITH: You ok?

EVE: Give her some space. What's your name darlin'?

EMILIA2: Emilia.

MARY: You aint from round here are you?

EMILIA2: Bishopsgate.

All the women react with an 'ooooh'

HESTER: What was so bad you wanted to throw yourself in there then?

FLORA: Your husband knocking you about?

JUDITH: Bankrupted you?

MARY: Got yourself pregnant?

EMILIA2: No.

EVE: Well then what you got to worry about with such lovely clothes?

HESTER: Filthy though. You don't want to walk back to Bishopsgate like that.

FLORA: Come with us and we'll sort you out.

EMILIA2: Oh no I couldn't possibly.

MARY: Hark at her! 'Couldn't possibly'! Why you putting on all them airs and graces?

EVE: Come with us luvvie. We'll clean you up.

EMILIA2: What are we doing?

JUDITH: We're having a steam up.

FLORA: Oh you'll love it. We'll make you feel brand new.

They arrive at the bath house. Much to EMILIA2's unease they go about undressing and washing her. They take her corset off and they wash her face. They find her clean clothes – they are simple and no corsetting.

JUDITH: This is all we have. Not as lovely as your dress I'm afraid.

EMILIA2. It's fine.

JUDITH: We'll get your under clothes washed up for you and sent on if you have some coin.

EMILIA2: Thank you.

MARY: Your lovely dress just needs drying and brushing off.

EMILIA2: No need.

EVE: Why not?

EMILIA2: I don't want it.

HESTER: Can we have it?

EMILIA2: Yeh.

The women fall on the clothes and corset and all end up with part of her clothes.

MARY: You sure you don't want all this?

EMILIA2: Take them as my thanks.

FLORA: It's no big thing missus. We fish someone out most days. Nice to be able to do it when they're still breathing.

JUDITH: Give her space. She looks peaky.

EMILIA2: I'm sorry.

HESTER: What you saying sorry for?

EMILIA2: Everything.

HESTER: What if we told you none of it was your fault?

EMILIA2: What?

HESTER: Whatever you were running from wasn't your fault.

EMILIA2: I think it was.

HESTER: Nah. It wasn't.

A pause.

EMILIA2: I don't know what I'm supposed to do.

EVE: You got any friends? Someone you can stay with? Or call on for anything?

EMILIA2: Yes.

LADY MARGARET CLIFFORD and her daughter LADY ANNE CLIFFORD step into sight. Music kicks in. EMILIA2 collapses in relief and either the CLIFFORDS or the RIVER WOMEN aid her on her journey

SCENE 2

She travels to the countryside. Music.

EMILIA3: It was like I had been given a single shard of light
to follow through a darkened room. The beam led me to
them. To the countryside, to the Cliffords.

EMILIA1: How had I let myself forget them before this?

EMILIA3: The warnings of Mary Sidney had blurred them
from my view perhaps? And just as waves take you out
to sea the waves can bring you back in. I felt a loss so
profound I was put to bed for several weeks. I was quite
unable to resist the weight of it. I could barely move,
let alone write. I could barely speak. I had sunk deeply
beneath the surface and nothing but time would heal
me. And why did I dream of my father? Every night? He
came. And I felt seven years old again. Everything begins
with death.

*She is approached by LADY ANNE who reads from Ovid's
Metamorphoses.*

LADY ANNE: At night the queen, arrayed to celebrate
The rites, went forth with frenzy's weaponry.
Vines wreathed her head, a light spear lay upon
Her shoulder and a deerskin draped her side.
Wild with her troop of women through the woods
She rushed, a sight of terror, frenzied by
The grief that maddened her, the image of
A real Bacchanal. At last she reached
The lonely hut and, screaming Bacchic cries,
Broke down the door, burst in and seized her sister,
Garbed her in Bacchic gear and hid her face,
Concealed in ivy leaves, and brought the girl
Back, in a daze, inside her palace wall.

LADY ANNE looks up from the book.

Will they kill Tereus? For what he did?

EMILIA2: They will do worse.

LADY ANNE: I like it. I like that they rescue her. Procne takes her band of women and hunts for her.

EMILIA2: And it is thanks to the embroidery Philomela wove that they learn the truth.

LADY ANNE: When you first came here all you had with you was what you had written.

EMILIA2: Yes.

LADY ANNE: Will you let me read it one day?

EMILIA2: I will.

LADY ANNE: You did not speak. It was as if your tongue had been cut out too.

EMILIA2: I was not as wretched as Philomela. Poor woman had been raped and had her tongue cut out with a sword. I can't pretend to have been treated as badly as that.

LADY ANNE: There is no competition to be had in all this though is there?

EMILIA2: You're too young to know that.

LADY ANNE: I've seen a lot. Are there any women in Greek myths who don't get raped or brutally mutilated or killed?

EMILIA2: Not many but we'll hunt them out.

LADY ANNE: I know about Clytemnestra and Medea and they are fearsome but not very nice.

EMILIA2: No.

Enter LADY MARGARET

LADY ANNE: Do women who get power have to be cruel as well?

EMILIA2: No they don't.

LADY ANNE: I want to read stories about that.

EMILIA2: Then we will have to write some.

LADY MARGARET: Shall we stop there?

LADY ANNE: Please say I make a good pupil! Please say you will continue.

EMILIA2: You are a very good pupil. But Margaret do you truly want someone like me to teach her?

LADY MARGARET: Someone like you? I would say that a woman who has learnt to think for herself would be the perfect kind of teacher for my daughter.

EMILIA2: It's not the conventional view.

LADY MARGARET: We are not conventional women.

EMILIA2: Thank you.

LADY ANNE: So you'll do it?

EMILIA2: How can I possibly refuse?

LADY MARGARET: Ok enough now. Let's not exhaust her, Anne. Please leave us a while.

LADY ANNE goes to leave then remembers she should curtsy which she does before running off.

Can I ask you something?

EMILIA2: Anything.

LADY MARGARET: When you were at court what knew you of my husband George?

EMILIA2: I regret, not much.

LADY MARGARET: You do not have to hide anything from me. I know most of his indiscretions but I am curious what those at court know.

EMILIA2: I've not been welcome at court for some time. But I know he had an appetite.

LADY MARGARET: Yes.

EMILIA2: And that he was less than discreet.

LADY MARGARET: And that I am a fool!

EMILIA2: No!

LADY MARGARET: I am! And people see me like one. He has shamed me and he has broken our marriage vows. He has taken what he wanted and he has forsaken all I have. How could he?

EMILIA2: Most easily my Lady. Because it is their right.

LADY MARGARET: By whose laws?

EMILIA2: Their own. Though madam as you know I have done it myself.

LADY MARGARET: But it didn't end well for you. It won't so much as touch George. It will be shrugged away. And yet here I am torn in two. I cannot do anything about it. But you can. Will you write something? For women. To warn us.

EMILIA2: What will I warn them of?

LADY MARGARET: Snakes.

EMILIA2: And how do I write about such things? To warn them of their tricks? Even if I had the means to publish women are only permitted by the censor to write of religion.

LADY MARGARET: We will find a way. But for now. Will you start writing? For yourself, as well as me? We need you to. We want you to. Please.

EMILIA2: Who am I to do this?

LADY MARGARET: You are my friend.

EMILIA2: Then I will.

LADY MARGARET kisses her and leaves.

EMILIA3: It was here wasn't it?

EMILIA1: Yes.

EMILIA3: Here that I began to think that perhaps I wasn't quite done yet. It is a wondrous thing when someone instills their confidence in you. Offers you their hand. Believes you can do it and you alone. Sees you not as a risk or a trifle, sees you not to be patronised or dismissed. And I see through my many years now how valuable that is to any kind of creation. And how lucky some have been to have had that from birth. An assumption that 'you will', instead of one that says 'you shouldn't'. I was lucky in that moment to feel it right then.

Over the following we see what she describes.

EMILIA1: I began to write short poems with, at first, subtle warnings and instruction to women on how to approach marriage. I would have Anne and Margaret read them and then they would copy them and pass them quietly to friends. What started small became steadily bigger. One or two copies became ten or twenty. They would be passed amongst us so many times they'd often return in several, tattered pieces. But of course it would only be a matter of time before one of them would fall into the wrong hands. In this instance my dear friend Lady Katherine's husband Sir Thomas Howard...

SCENE 3

SIR THOMAS HOWARD and LADY KATHERINE arrive. He is furious. LADY MARGARET and LADY ANNE receive them.

LORD HOWARD: Out of the way, very important man coming through. Dear Countess I apologise for coming here with little warning. I'm afraid I was compelled to come after experiencing something so vile and so terrible that I wanted to be sure you knew who exactly you were harbouring.

LADY MARGARET: Whatever could you mean Sir Thomas??

EMILIA2 enters

LORD HOWARD: This...well I can hardly call her Lady...this female...

LADY MARGARET: Sir Thomas I ask you to explain your manner it is most out of place.

LORD HOWARD: Emilia Lanier is a danger to us all.

LADY MARGARET: Oh heavens! How so?

LORD HOWARD: Not only does she shame both her husband and herself in a most public display of vulgarity on the stage. But are you aware of the fact that she seems to be producing notelets of filth which encourage the most base and disreputable behaviour amongst fine lady folk as yourself?

LADY MARGARET: Are you talking about her poems?

LORD HOWARD: You've seen them?

LADY MARGARET: Of course! I've helped to reproduce and pass them round.

LORD HOWARD: *(Incredulous.)* Reproduce?!

LADY MARGARET: To be frank with you Sir Thomas they really aren't meant for you to read. They're for a Lady's eyes only. And they're not as bad as you seem to be making out. But I suppose while we have you here it would be good to get your opinion. I know Emilia would appreciate the feedback. Did you like them?

LORD HOWARD: Like them? LIKE THEM?! They are the most revolting and insidiously terrifying things I have ever had the displeasure of reading!

LADY MARGARET: Not your cup of tea then.

LORD HOWARD: No! And I am shocked and appalled at your lack of outrage about the matter. Are you not revolted by them too? They speak of Adam being at fault and not Eve. *(Reading.)* 'But surely Adam can not be excus'd, her fault, though great, yet hee was most too blame' They call men vipers. They debase the very souls who support and give them permission to live upon gods good earth. Instead of giving thanks for the generous and kind disposition of all men she seems to suggest that men are to be ignored and discarded in favour of a new order in which women are seen as equal. This preposterous notion gives no thought to clear fact that for as long as time immemorial women have never been equal to men and instead must accept the natural order of things. Inferior. Ever more so and subservient to the end! This poetry, if you can call it that, is akin to a call to arms and it is the most dangerous rubbish I've ever read. Can you imagine if all women came to believe what she suggests? That women deserve more than they already generously are given? Can you imagine the horror of that? Well I can and I will not stand for this. Which is why I am here and why I say to you Emilia Lanier you will desist your terrible actions and if you do not you will find yourself in a most destitute position. No one at court will entertain you. No patronage will ever come your way. Be mindful of the fact your husband right now is seeking a knighthood for his part in the battles being waged and it would reflect very badly for you both if you did not hush your tongue and stay your pen. Just think on that. Do not forget the growing discomfort at the spread of a certain kind of sorcery that this could be described as. You would not want to be tried as a witch Emilia – I fear your crimes would not go down well. And Lady Margaret I thought better of you. I hope you will reconsider housing such a criminal as this.

LADY MARGARET: Are you quite done?

LORD HOWARD: Why yes!

LADY MARGARET: Good. Lady Katherine do you have anything to say?

LORD HOWARD: No she does not! She is in complete agreement with me.

LADY MARGARET: I asked your good Lady wife.

LORD HOWARD: And she does not need to reply when I have done it for her.

LADY MARGARET: Would you let her speak?

LADY KATHERINE: I am in agreement with my husband.

LORD HOWARD: You see?

LADY KATHERINE: I hope that my friend Emilia will see sense and stop this action of hers as it does tarnish the rest of us so terribly.

EMILIA2: Kate surely you can agree this is all a bit ridiculous. Witch craft?

LADY KATHERINE: You would do well to heed my husband's advice.

LADY MARGARET: Well it's hardly advice. It was a threat!
A terrible one. How dare you come to my home and
threaten my guests so!

EMILIA2: It's alright Countess.

LADY MARGARET: No it is not. I would ask that they leave now.

LORD HOWARD: I will report back to your husband how
foolish his wife has been.

LADY MARGARET: You can tell that bastard what a fool I think
he is!

LADY ANNE: *(Thrilled.)* Mother!

LORD HOWARD: I have never heard such crass and terrible
language from one that would call herself a Lady!

LADY MARGARET: Oh get out you old turd.

LADY ANNE: Both of you! Out!

LORD HOWARD: Disrespectful!

*LORD HOWARD and LADY KATHERINE are sent packing. LADY
MARGARET and ANNE are flushed and excited by the encounter.
EMILIA2 is quiet.*

LADY MARGARET: The cheek of it!

LADY ANNE: Mother you were wonderful!

LADY MARGARET: I rather was wasn't I? What a horrible man.
But we must not be deterred.

EMILIA2: And yet we should be. His threat is a very real one.

LADY MARGARET: Emilia he is scared. They all are.

EMILIA2: Yes.

LADY MARGARET: All that talk of 'witch craft' for heavens sake.

EMILIA2: I know.

LADY MARGARET: Do not be deterred.

SCENE 4

They disperse. A musical note. Everyone focuses on EMILIA3

EMILIA3: Search for this now and you won't see it. Look for this in words and it won't be there. Almost nothing is kept. Nothing is remembered. But in our muscles we feel it. Memories of intention. Memories of need and fury and pain. We hear the echoes bouncing down the passage of time and into our dreams. We read what was recorded and we see what is missing. We see what they did not want us to write down.

Time passes.

EMILIA2 is home with ALPHONSO

EMILIA2: Husband.

ALPHONSO: Wife.

EMILIA2: You really fucked it didn't you?

ALPHONSO: As did you.

EMILIA2: We have nothing?

ALPHONSO: Well...

EMILIA2: No knighthood despite it all?

ALPHONSO: I'm afraid not.

EMILIA2: Then we must get creative.

ALPHONSO: I don't want to die a pauper!

EMILIA2: You need to find a way to earn more money.

ALPHONSO: What can I do?

EMILIA2: Find a way to return to court and play again.

ALPHONSO: Oh heavens alive are you insane? I haven't picked up a recorder since my glory days in Elizabeth's reign. I wouldn't know what to do with the damn thing. Let's be honest I am exceedingly low on all skills.

EMILIA2: You need to find something.

ALPHONSO: I can't go back to earning a pittance, it will hardly keep us.

EMILIA2: Well luckily you won't be the only one earning.

ALPHONSO: How so?

EMILIA2: I'm going to teach.

ALPHONSO: Oh good! Do you have another rich bitch from court needing their idiot children integrated into humanity?

EMILIA2: No. I'm going to teach women from over the bridge.

ALPHONSO: South of the river?

EMILIA2: Yes. I understand women aren't generally on your radar but even you must have noticed a great many of them have had little to no access to any education ever.

ALPHONSO: How in the hell will you make any money from doing that?

EMILIA2: Whatever they can afford I will ask for.

ALPHONSO: Oh lord you think you're Jesus. The Mary Magdalen's of Bankside will lap it up. And how do you think you teaching whores and fish wives their ABC's is going to help our standing?

EMILIA2: I don't care.

ALPHONSO: Pardon?

EMILIA2: I no longer care about our standing.

ALPHONSO: Well when we're languishing in the gutter it will serve you well to 'not care' about what people think of you.

EMILIA2: Alphonso, I want to change things. You of all people must long for things to change.'

ALPHONSO: What is that supposed to mean?

EMILIA2: If things were different wouldn't you have been happier?

ALPHONSO: I don't know.

EMILIA2: In many ways we're very alike.

ALPHONSO: You have not made me unhappy. If anything it's been rather fun getting news of what you've been up to.

EMILIA2: I'll be careful.

ALPHONSO: Clever woman.

He leaves.

EMILIA3: So what did I do? I started to teach.

SCENE 5

1610

Music. The River Women burst onto stage, loud and boisterous. MARY, EVE, JUDITH, FLORA and HESTER.

MARY: Emilia! Sorry we're late. Something happened down at the docks and we had to rubber neck.

JUDITH: Broken down cart...

HESTER: Manure flippin' everywhere...

EVE: Women screaming about her lost sheep

JUDITH: And some Idiot man trying to beat up the statue of the king.

FLORA: Just the usual.

JUDITH: Yeh but I heard that the woman was screaming because she was being dragged off on charges of witchcraft.

FLORA: *(Shocked.)* She wasn't!

EVE: It's so hysterical. I wish they'd stop with all that nonsense.

JUDITH: It's terrifying is what it is.

HESTER: I don't like the way things are going at all.

MARY: Yeh and if they saw what you do with the devil you'll be up in flames before you know it!

HESTER: Oi! Please respect my privacy – me and the devil have a very respectable thing going on. Anyway. I've brought the coin I owe you from last time Emilia, and what I owe you for today. I've had a good week at the Dirty Dick so I'm flush.

EVE: I bet you have you filthy Danish bitch! You and the devil living it up!

HESTER: Serving! I was serving!

MARY : I bet you were you filthy bitch!

The women laugh.

HESTER: Oh fucksake! Tell them Emilia, they won't be ladies if their minds are in the gutters.

EMILIA2: Ok settle down. Have you all had a chance to read what I gave you last time?

EVE: Oh about that. I did read it but my husband found it and used it on the pot.

JUDITH: He wiped his arse with her poem? The dirty bastard!

MARY: That's pure disrespect that is!

EMILIA2: I'm not a stranger to bad reviews. But we all know those poems aren't meant for your husbands. What did you think of it before you lost it?

EVE: I liked it.

EMILIA2: Did you?

EVE: Yeh. I did.

(She quotes.)

You came not in the world without our paine,
Make that a barre against your crueltie;
Your fault beeing greater, why should you disdaine
Our beeing your equals, free from tyranny?

The women react.

Now that is good. Speaks to us all. And do you know what? It inspired me to write my own.

EMILIA2: Really?

EVE: Shall I read it?

EMILIA2: Please.

The other women woop and cheer.

EVE: Alright. Here we go. Be kind.
>Where are you going you horrible bastard?
>You owe me coin for that trick
>Don't you run from me if you know what's good for you
>I'll make a tree of you with this stick
>I don't care how much you hit me
>My husband does it so much I'm blue
>But if you take my coin I'll kill ya
>That's just what a girls gotta do.
>Thank you.

The women applaud and cheer.

EMILIA2: My goodness. You were inspired by my poem to write that?

EVE: Well look, you talk of making sure you have ways of keeping valuable things to yourself. Like jewels and clothes. So your husband can't spend everything you own. Which is canny and good advice. Except I aint never had no jewels and the only clothes I own are the ones I'm wearing and aint no one paying me nothing for these old shitty rags so I thought to myself – what's the equivalent?

MARY: Ooooh girl!

HESTER: Equivalent!

EVE: Yeh I went there! New word!

EMILIA2: Well done for using it correctly.

EVE: Thanks miss. So yeh. What's the equivalent – and I was like, well for me it's when I turn tricks and the bastard doesn't pay me so I got to beat him til he does and then I put the coin somewhere my husband aint gonna find it.

JUDITH: Up her...

EVE: Yeh mate. And then I wrote this.

JUDITH: It's mint.

EVE: Thank you.

JUDITH: I liked the bit about the tree. Well descriptive.

EVE: Thanks babe.

JUDITH: I ain't written nothing but I read yours and it's alright you know.

EMILIA2: Thank you.

MARY: Yeh I liked it too. I read it out loud and my mum said I sounded like a posh bitch and I liked that. Ere Miss. Can we ask you something?

EMILIA2: Of course.

MARY: We heard a rumour about you. Did you and Will Shakespeare used to...you know?

JUDITH: You can't just ask her that!

MARY: What?

JUDITH: That's personal for a lady. She aint like you or I.

EVE: It aint like it's not common knowledge though.

EMILIA2: What isn't?

EVE: About you and him.

EMILIA2: Really?

EVE: Yeh! You are her aintcha?

EMILIA2: Who?

HESTER: The one in the sonnets. The 'dark lady'. It's got to be you.

EMILIA2: What sonnets?

HESTER: Oh you haven't seen them yet? They're being passed round still, I'll try and get you them.

FLORA reluctantly looks for her copy knowing the contents of them.

MARY: How was it? 'My mistress' eyes are nothing like the sun'

JUDITH: 'Coral is far more red than her lips' red.

MARY: 'If snow be white, why then her breasts are dun'

EVE: 'If hairs be wires, black wires grow on her head.'

EMILIA2: 'I have seen roses damask;d, red and white, But no such roses see I in her cheeks'

HESTER: You have read them!

EMILIA2: Many years ago.

EVE: See! I told you it was her!

EMILIA2: It could be any number of women. I wasn't the only one.

FLORA: Here!

She finds a little book of sonnets and passes them to EMILIA2 who starts flicking through them.

EVE: I mean they're super passionate. "Thou art the fairest and most precious jewel." And rather lovely. For the most.

JUDITH: But they get pretty brutal. "For I have sworn thee fair, and thought thee bright, Who art as black as hell, as dark as night." I mean you clearly broke his heart.

MARY: Maybe she shouldn't read them.

EMILIA2: How could he?

MARY: Maybe they're not about you after all?

EMILIA2: How could he do this?

FLORA: They're probably some other dark lady.

EMILIA2: I remember him writing them. They were for us. Not for the world to see. He published them?

JUDITH: Looks like it.

EMILIA2: Again he takes everything and leaves me nothing. Why can I not be free of him? He takes my name and runs it through the mud for his own gain.

EVE: To be fair he doesn't name you.

EMILIA2: But you knew it. Did you not? How?

EVE: Literally everyone is talking about it.

EMILIA2: I feel like I've lost everything again. Will this be how I am remembered? My name on their lips? Is there anything more violating?

None of the women know what to say.

I'm sorry. Look at me. Self pity for something so trivial.

MARY: It's not trivial.

EMILIA2: It is. When I know what you all face every day I have nothing to be complaining about.

JUDITH: If he's hurt you then he's hurt you and there's nothing more to say. Come 'ere darlin'

She pulls her in for a hug.

EMILIA3: Oh those women. What they taught me. When they brought me into their world. The days we had together. The time we spent.

EMILIA1: Are you ready now?

EMILIA3: Just wait one moment more.

SCENE 6

ALPHONSO arrives.

ALPHONSO: Even when they had you in make up and skirts you somehow wore your difference with a kind of pride.

EMILIA2: Are you alright?

ALPHONSO: You and I never really fitted in did we?

EMILIA2: Alphonso.

ALPHONSO: You let me be.

EMILIA2: And you I. What is this about? I need to get on.

ALPHONSO: We were born in the wrong time you know?

EMILIA2: Actually maybe this was the perfect time for us.

ALPHONSO: Clever woman.

He starts walking away.

EMILIA2: *(Calling out to him, confused.)* Hey! We're not done. Where are you going? Alphonso?

ALPHONSO exits. EMILIA2 watches, confused by his leaving suddenly.

MARY: Emilia love? You been out all day? I've got some sad news.

JUDITH: Emilia? You haven't heard have you? Sorry to have to tell you this.

EVE: Sorry you have to hear from me.

FLORA: I didn't want you going back there and finding him.

HESTER: It's your husband love. He's dead.

MARY: Can we do anything to help you?

HESTER: Is she alright?

EVE: It's the shock aint it?

FLORA: When my husband died I was ecstatic.

JUDITH: Nice word.

FLORA: Ta. But I guess Emilia liked hers.

Two MEN appear. They are dressed well and obviously have money.

MAN 1: Hello darlins

MAN 2: Got some time for us?

MARY: Not now mate!

JUDITH: Sod off.

MAN 2: *(To FLORA.)* What about you?

FLORA: You're pissed. Go away.

MAN 1: Charming!

MAN 2: Nasty little bitches don't want our money.

MAN 1: If you learnt some manners you could have earned
    yourselves a decent whack tonight.

EVE: We don't want your money, you heard them; piss off.

MAN 2: You watch your filthy mouth.

MAN 1: You don't know who we are – we can have you strung
    up and thrown in the tower.

MAN 2: We could have you burnt at the goddamn stake.

HESTER: You're drunk. Go home.

MAN 2: YOU DON'T GET TO TELL US WHAT TO DO.

MAN 1: If we wanted you we could have you.

HESTER: Don't test us.

MAN 1: Or what?

No response.

OR WHAT?

He goes up to EMILIA2

MAN 2: What's your problem eh? Pretty little Moor. Where you from then eh? You know you'd be a lot prettier if you smiled. Go on darlin' crack one out for me. Might never happen. What's wrong with her? Is it that time of the month? Where are you from you miserable cow? Can't she speak English? Tell her I said she's a miserable cow.

Something visceral snaps within the EMILIAS and a roar comes out of her before they launch on the men. A big cathartic fight ensues.

MAN 1: She's insane!

MAN 2: Witchcraft! The devil in her!

MAN 1: This is the devil's work!

HESTER: Go! GO!

EMILIA1: Now?

EMILIA3: NOW!

The MEN run off and the women envelope EMILIA2 who has collapsed. EMILIA3 launches into the next scene.

SCENE 7

EMILIA3: Men, who forgetting they were borne of women, nourished of women, and that if it were not by the meanes of women, they would be quite extinguished out of the

world, and a finall ende of them all, doe like Vipers deface
the wombes wherein they were bred, onely to give way
and utterance to their want of discretion and goodnesse.
Therefore we are not to regard any imputations, that they
undeservedly lay upon us, no otherwise than to make use
of them to our owne benefits, as spurres to vertue, making
us flie all occasions that may colour their unjust speeches
to pass currant.

EVE: Who wrote that?

EMILIA3: I did!

*LADY KATHERINE enters with LADY ANNE. KATHERINE is badly beaten
and her face is bruised and bloody. She stands proudly in front of
EMILIA3 holding her composure.*

LADY KATHERINE: My dear Emilia. You were hard to find.

EMILIA3: Katherine? Your face! Anne.

LADY KATHERINE: I'm sorry I've come in a state of disrepair.

EMILIA3: You don't need to be so formal with me Kate. What
happened?

LADY KATHERINE: My husband.

EMILIA3: Lord Howard did this? Why? He did this because of
my words?

LADY KATHERINE: Your beautiful, brilliant words! Those
poems have been the most perfect morsels of truth
and every new one that came would fill me with such
happiness and gratitude that there was someone out there
who knew me somehow. And when I found out it was you
that was writing them I was so proud. And I wanted to tell
you so but I've been too stubborn and stupid to do it. And
scared. But I am proud. And I'm sorry I ever tried to stop
you.

74

EMILIA3: You are not stupid Katherine. It is because of her sense and foresight that her husband is as rich as he is. Your skills have benefited him greatly and this is how he repays you? How long has it been going on?

LADY KATHERINE: From the very start. I have been so cruel to you when all you were asking me was for my support. Will you keep showing them that we talk? Will you keep showing them that we can function as they wish us to but behind closed doors like these right now, we talk. I want them to realise this. And I want them to be as scared as I have been my whole life. And I want you to show them that we can do what they do despite their best efforts to stop us. I want to do now what I should have done a long time ago. Let me help you publish your work.

EMILIA3: Publish? We'll never get them past the censor.

LADY ANNE: So you change them. Just like we change our very natures for them you can change your words. Course you can! We do it without even thinking it don't we? We barely even blink. We know from the moment we're born that we must become shapeshifters and tricksters. That what we wear as our outer skin, our masks, are there to shield what we have kicking and tearing inside us. This world works against us but we're like some kind of wily upstream swimmers, jumping and diving. We're born with it. If we're lucky, like I was, our mothers teach us it. We know what to do. You know exactly what to do; think round it. What can women write? What will get past the censor?

EMILIA3: Religious texts.

LADY ANNE: Write a religious text but inside it, deep inside what you write, place your messages for us. We who have read your poems will know what you are saying to us. The censor won't suspect a thing.

EMILIA3: Clever woman.

LADY ANNE: I had a great teacher.

FLORA: I know a publisher. If the money is right he'll print anything.

LADY KATHERINE: Leave the money to me and Lady Margaret Clifford – we'll write to the women of court who loved your words. I'm sure they'll help. Lead the way my dear.

FLORA: We can talk to him. He owes me.

FLORA and LADY KATHERINE leave together. EMILIA3 is half way between the memory and now.

EMILIA3: Teach. Teaching. Words. On a page. This was our chance. This is what we'd been waiting for. We publish my poems. Properly. Officially. As well as that. We realised we could go further. This moment. I remember this. Search for this now and you won't find it. So many of us were fighting to work, to be chartered, to be recognised. We were part of that. This is what I said – Do you know what I'm thinking? When I take my poems to the men in the scriptorium to copy for our lessons, I give them our money. I give them coin to copy my words. They are making copies, writing letters, contracts, creating pamphlets. With everything I've taught you. You can do what they do.

HESTER: A scriptorium?

EMILIA3: We do the copying. We do the writing. We make the money. Anne let's make what we made before but bigger. More advice, no censors, what we can't publish in my book of poems we put in a pamphlet to distribute far and wide.

LADY ANNE: It's dangerous.

EMILIA3: Yes it is dangerous.

She looks around her for agreement.

MARY: Let's get to work.

SCENE 8

Music. High tempo. Exciting. Fun. Women coming together. Everyone rushes to action. Over the following EMILIA's scriptorium is formed. Pamphlets are made and distributed out to the audience. 'If you want to keep your money don't marry' 'if you marry keep a stash of your own' ' remember if you're widowed you gain rights you never had before'. Sections of Emilia's own poetry. EMILIA3 directs action. The women help write and distribute the pamphlets. LADY KATHERINE helps to gain patronage from other monied women. Once done HESTER bursts in.

HESTER: The women of the town are loving the pamphlets! We're getting involved. There are protests planned. The women are hopeful their voices will be heard.

JUDITH: We need a run of fifty of this pamphlet ladies, as we ran out too quickly last week. There's still space for a short poem on the final page. Does anyone have anything they wish to contribute.

MARY: Eve does!

EVE: No I don't!

MARY: You do! You said you had finished one last night and you were waiting to see if there would be space.

EVE: Well I aint so sure anymore.

EMILIA3: Read it to us.

EVE: No bleedin' way.

EMILIA3: Eve you won't know if it's any good if you don't let us hear it.

77

EVE: And I wont' know if it's awful if I don't too.

MARY: No one won a war like that.

EVE: We aint at war.

EMILIA3: Oh yes we are. Read it.

EVE: I can't.

EMILIA3: Then I will.

She holds out her hand and EVE reluctantly hands her the poem.

There is volume in my silence
If you stop to listen
Look into my eyes and you will
Hear quite clearly what i'm trying to say
Be careful, I am saying
Be careful
What you have taken is not yours
And one day, loudly, I shall take it back.

The women take it in.

MARY: It doesn't rhyme.

EMILIA3: It's perfect. Put it on the final page. On it's own. It needs a whole page of it's own. What do you think?

EVE: My poem next to yours? It would be an honour.

FLORA: Emilia! Your books are ready!

The muses arrive with the books. Ends with EMILIA3 hugging her newly printed book to her chest. The women disperse. Except EVE who remains watching EMILIA3.

EMILIA3: I found myself marvelling at where I had started and where I was now. From such beginnings as I had come from, the paths I had chosen and the paths I had not. The many moments of change that had shaped me. Forever on a page. Forever on a shelf. Forever to be read by enquiring eyes and minds. And yet. If I could only freeze this moment before it happened I would.

She looks at EVE who nods and turns and leaves.

But here it comes.

The building of music and beat. FLORA comes running on.

FLORA: Emilia! Oh god help us. Emilia!

EMILIA3: This is what happens when we speak.

FLORA: Eve. It's Eve. They've got her.

EMILIA3: When we do not cut out our tongues.

FLORA: They found her with the pamphlets. They said it was the devils work.

We see EVE being placed on a pyre. Music. Build. Horror and sadness.

EMILIA3: When we do not stay silent. This is what they do. This is what they did. Our Eve. Our Eve. They took our Eve.

While she speaks we see EVE go up in flames.

And we could not go to her like Procne went to her sister. We could not go with frenzy's weaponry to scream Bacchic cries of anguish and break down the door to seize our sister. We could not go.

A song for EVE. There is the sense that the party is over. Everything she was celebrating has now been forgotten. The reality of their lives, too dark. EMILIA3 is left alone.

SCENE 9

SHAKESPEARE arrives.

EMILIA3: You died long ago old man.

SHAKESPEARE: You'll be dead soon too, old woman.

EMILIA3: Why are you here?

SHAKESPEARE: Well I'm widely regarded as the greatest writer in English Language, a national treasure and the worlds most famous playwright so any theatre I may step into can legitimately be considered 'My gaff'.

EMILIA3: Not right now it isn't.

SHAKESPEARE: You had fun?

EMILIA3: It's a nice feeling isn't it? When you see them watching. Knowing your words are sitting within them now. That perhaps you took them on a journey. Perhaps you let them have some time away from themselves to understand you just a little.

SHAKESPEARE: I never wrote for people to understand me. I wrote to understand them.

EMILIA3: You never understood me though did you?

SHAKESPEARE: No. Perhaps. A little.

EMILIA3: What did you know of me?

SHAKESPEARE: That you were from a musical family. Italian. Jewish probably but you hid it. And likely of North African Descent. That you were passionate. That you loved to write. That you were more intelligent than many of the people around you would give you credit for. That you were hot. That you were a good mother and grandmother, or at least you wanted to be. That you were

EMILIA3: Stifled. Ignored. Abused.

SHAKESPEARE: That you weren't the first and you wouldn't be the last. That you spoke for many who could not speak. That you must have been so brave to have done what you did. That you deserve all of this right now. That perhaps you even knew that one day this would happen for you. That when things started to shift you would emerge. That you would be able to give something hundreds of years after you died. After you were buried by history. I think you probably knew all this. Or at least hoped. That the time would one day be right.

EMILIA3: Yeh.

SHAKESPEARE: Clever woman.

EMILIA3: Yeh I am.

He goes.

SCENE 10

She takes a moment to regard us all.

EMILIA3: What can I say to you? Now. What. Can I. I want to tell you about anger. Because it is not just something that passes through like a storm. It is something that forms the core of me. Like the earth has the heat of its origins deep in it's centre I do too. I have been told that my anger is not to be seen on my outside. That it is not seemly. It doesn't help. I have been told, even by other women, that it detracts from what I have tried to say. I have been told that it's distracting people from moving forward as they are too consumed by the guilt I am giving them. And that my hatred of the men whose very ills fuel this anger, detracts from my arguments. But you say we hate men as if we silence them, as if we beat and abuse them, rape them, as if we shame them for their desires, as if we restrict them from any kind of independence and agency. As if we hang them and drown them and stone them and burn them. I am 76 years old and I hold in me a muscle memory of every woman who came before me and I will send more for those that will come after. For Eve. For every Eve. I don't know if you can feel it. Do you? Do you feel it? Inside of you. You don't need to be a woman to know what is coming. Because why have our stories been ignored? For so long? Ask yourself why.

A rumble is approaching. Drums.

Listen to us. Listen to every woman who came before you. Listen to every woman with you now. And listen when I say to you to take the fire as your own. That anger that you feel it is yours and you can use it. We want you to. We need you to. Look how far we've come already. Don't stop now. The house that has been built around you is not made of stone. The stakes we have been tied to will not survive if our flames burn bright. And if they try to burn you, may your fire be stronger than theirs so you can burn the whole fucking house down.

A song, a dance, a celebration.

END

Introduction to the Poems

In August 2017 I had my first cup of coffee with Michelle Terry who had recently been announced as the next artistic director of The Globe. When I arrived it was she that told me all about Emilia Bassano. Told me of a woman forgotten by history who was one of the best cases for being the 'Dark Lady of The Sonnets' and therefore potentially Shakespeare's lover but also a woman who was a talented writer herself, a mother and feminist of the time. Someone who somehow had the wherewithal to publish her poems and therefore is regarded as one of the first English woman to do so. Someone who perhaps knew that if she didn't publish she stood no chance of ever being remembered. When Michelle told me about her I remember a shared astonishment at the fact she was so unknown. But at the same time a recognition of why. A woman whose voice has been ignored for so long? A woman whose talent has been ignored? A woman who probably voiced concerns at her lack of opportunity and was dismissed and therefore had to take matters into her own hands? A woman only remembered as the potential lover and maybe even 'baby mother' of the most famous playwright in history? A woman who juggled writing, love, children and life? A woman. A woman and her story untold. It all felt not only recognisable but relevant.

When I began researching with my wonderful director Nicole Charles we realised how little there was written about her and that what had been written was not necessarily reliable. As with most historical interpretations there isn't much to go on and it entirely depended on who was analysing what there was. Many historians who had written about her had formed an opinion on her based on the writings of Simon Forman who she visited as her astrologer and a kind of counsellor. He recorded their sessions. On the one hand it's a valuable document and if it didn't exist perhaps we would not know anything at all about Emilia. On the other hand we found it very hard to believe every word he wrote. He openly admits that she wouldn't have sex with him (which seemed to be something he tried to do with many of his female clients) and the bitterness shines through many of his descriptions of her.

> "*She was maintained in great pomp. She is high-minded – she hath £40 a year and was wealthy to him that married her, in money and jewels. She can hardly keep secret. She was very brave in youth. She hath many false conceptions. She hath a son, his name is Henry*'. Later on her writes of her '*shows the woman hath a mind to the quent, but seems she is or will be a harlot. And because…she useth sodomy.*' And ' *She was a whore and dealt evil with him after*'. And '*to know why Mrs Lanier sent for me; what will follow, and whether she intendeth any more villainy*'.

We found it very hard to take much of what he said about her seriously and in fact we were pretty angry that his words have come to be so important in the retelling of her story for so many. For so many people of that era it would have been impossible to make a mark and be remembered. They didn't record things like we do now. There was no such thing as a diarist. People didn't journal. Notes and pamphlets and letters definitely circulated but they would be read and discarded – used to line a drawer or wipe a bum. To survive and be remembered as 'someone' your relevance and achievements needed to be published. Our version of Emilia knew this. Our version recognised that if she was going to be remembered she needed to publish her poems. Which she did. Not many original copies exist and the more recent publication of them by AL Rowse unfortunately includes a lot of what Simon Forman said about her in the introduction. I wanted to re-publish some of her poems with the play to hopefully give them exposure through a different lens.

Our Emilia was fiercely intelligent, a writer, a survivor, a fighter, a mother and an educator. We know from court records that she set up a school for girls, that she fought for inheritance owed, that she lived to the ripe old age of seventy-six, that she birthed two children, lost one as a baby and many others as miscarriages. That she was the daughter of migrants from Italy and would have suffered prejudice and injustice. That she wrote many poems that she published and no doubt wrote many more. That she knew that to be published as a woman she needed to get past the censor and write religious poetry and within it she hid messages for her fellow woman. To challenge the normal narratives. To challenge their oppressors. To not be deterred. Our Emilia spoke through the ages to us and we hope we have done her proud with this play. She's our hero. And I'm so glad we have been able to republish some of her amazing words alongside this play.

For every Emilia there are hundreds of other talents and voices lost to history. We must seek them out and amplify them. Let's stop re-reading the same old narratives…there are so many more out there we haven't heard yet.

MLM, July 2018

Poems

Often haue I heard that it is the property of some women, not only to emulate the virtues and perfections
of the rest, but also by all their powers of ill speaking,
to ecclipse the brightness of their deserued fame: now
contrary to this custome, which men I hope uniustly lay to
their charge, I haue written this small volume, or little booke,
for the generall vse of all virtuous Ladies and Gentlewomen
of this kingdome; and in commendation of some particular
persons of our owne sexe, such as for the most part, are so well
knowne to my selfe, and others, that I dare undertake Fame
dares not to call any better. And this haue I done, to make
knowne to the world, that all women deserue not to be blamed
though some forgetting they are women themselues, and in
danger to be condemned by the words of their owne mouthes,
fall into so great an errour, as to speake vnaduisedly against
the rest of their sexe; which if it be true, I am persuaded they
can shew their owne imperfection in nothing more: and therefore could wish (for their owne ease, modesties, and credit) they
would referre such points of folly, to be practised by euell dispo-
sed men, who forgetting they were borne of women, nourished
of women, and that if it were not by the means of women, they
would be quite extinguished out of the world: and a finall ende
of them all, doe like Vipers deface the wombes wherein they
were bred, onely to giue way and vtterance to their want of
discretion and goodnesse. Such as these, were they that disho-
noured Christ his Apostles and Prophets, putting them to
shamefull deaths. Therefore, we are not to regard any imputations that they vndeseruedly lay upon us, no otherwise than
to make vse of them to our owne benefits, as spurres to vertue, making vs flie all occasions that may colour their uniust
speeches to passe currant. Especially considering that they haue
tempted euen the patience of God himselfe, who gaue power to
wise and virtuous women, to bring downe their pride and ar-
rogancie. As was cruell Cesarus by the discreet counsell of noble Deborah, Iudge and Prophetesse of Israel: and resolution
of Jael wife of Heber the Kenite: wicket Haman, by the di-
uine prayers and prudent proceedings of beautiful Hester:
blasphemous Holofernes, by the inuincible courage, rare wis-

dome, and confident carriage of Iudeth: & the vniust Iudges, by the innocency of chast Susanna: with infinite others, which for breuitie sake I will omit. As also in respect it pleased our Lord and Sauiour Iesus Christ, without the assistance of man, beeing free from originall and all other sinnes, from the time of his conception, till the houre of his death, to be begotten of a woman, borne of a woman, nourished of a woman, obedient to a woman; and that he healed woman, pardoned women, comforted women: yea, euen when he was in his greatest agonie and bloodie sweat, going to be crucified, and also in the last houre of his death, tooke care to dispose of a woman: after his resurrection, appeared first to a woman, sent a woman to declare his most glorious resurrection to the rest of his Disciples. Many other examples I could alledge of diuers faithfull and virtuous women, who haue in all ages, not onely beene Confessors, but also indured most cruel martyrdome for their faith in Iesus Christ. All which is sufficient to inforce all good Christians and honourable minded men to speake reuerently of our sexe, and especially of all virtuous and good women. To the modest sensures of both which, I refer these my imperfect indeauours, knowing that according to their owne excellent dispositions, they will rather, cherish, nourish, and increase the least sparke of virtue where they find it, by their fauourable and beste interpretations, than quench it by wrong constructions. To whom I wish all increase of virtue, and desire their best opinions.

THE DESCRIPTION OF COOKE-HAM

Farewell (sweet Cooke ham) where I first obtain'd
Grace from that Grace where perfit Grace remain'd;
And where the Muses gaue their full consent,
I should haue powre the virtuous to content:
Where princely Palace will'd me to indite,
The sacred Storie of the Soules delight,
Farewell (sweet Place) where Virtue then did rest,
And all delights did harbour in her breast:
Never shall my sad eies againe behold
Those pleasures which my thoughts did then vnfold:
Yet you (great Lady) Mistris of that Place,
From whose desires did spring this worke of Grace;
Vouchsafe to think vpon those pleasures past
As fleeting worldly Ioyes that could not last:
Or, as dimme shadowes of celestiall pleasures,

Which are desir'd aboue all earthly treasures.
Oh how (me thought) against you thither came,
Each part did seeme some new delight to frame!
The House receiu'd all ornaments to grace it,
And would indure no foulenesse to deface it.
The Walkes put on their summer Liueries,
And all things else did hold like similies:
The Trees with leaues, with fruits, with flowers clad,
Embrac'd each other, seeming to be glad,
Turning themselues to beauteous Canopies,
To shade the bright Sunne from your brighter eies:
The cristall Streames with siluer spangles graced,
While by the glorious Sunne they were embraced:
The little Birds in chirping notes did sing,
To entertaine both You and that sweet Spring.
And Philomela with her sundry layes,
Both You and that delightfull Place did praise.
Oh how me thought each plant, each floure, each tree
Set forth their beauties then to welcome thee!
The very Hills right humbly did descend,
When you to tread vpon them did intend,
And as you set your feete, they still did rise,
Glad that they could receiue so rich a prise.
The gentle Windes did take delight to bee
Among those woods that were so grac'd by thee.
And in sad murmure vtterd pleasing sound,
That Pleasure in that place might more abound:
The swelling Bankes deliuer'd all their pride,
When such a Phoenix once they had espide.
Each Arbor, Banke, each Seate, each stately Tree,
Thought themselues honor'd in supporting thee.
The pretty Birds would oft come to attend thee,
Yet flie away for feare they should offend thee:
The little creatures in the Burrough by
Would come abraod to sport them in your eye;
Yet fearefull of the Bowe in your faire Hand
Would runne away when you did make a stand.
Now let me come vnto that stately Tree,
Wherein such goodly Prospects you did see;
That Oake that did in height his fellowes passe,
As much as lofty trees, low growing grasse:
Much like a comely Cedar streight and tall,
Whose beauteous stature farre exceeded all:
How often did you visite this faire tree,
Which seeming joyfull in receiuing thee,

Would like a Palme tree spread his armes abroad,
Desirous that you there should make abode:
Whose faire greene leaues much like a comely vaile,
Defended Phebus when he would assaile:
Whose pleasing boughes did yeeld a coole fresh ayre,
Ioying his happinesse when you were there.
Where beeing seated, you might plainely see,
Hills, vales, and woods, as if on bended knee
They had appeard, your honour to salute,
Or to preferre some strange vnlook'd for sute:
All interlac'd with brookes and christall springs,
A Prospect fit to please the eyes of Kings:
And thirteene shires appear'd all in your sight,
Europe could not affoard much more delight.
What was there then but gaue you all content,
While you the time in meditation spent,
Of their Creators powre, which there you saw,
In all his Creatures held a perfit Law;
And in their beauties did you plaine descrie,
His beauty, wisdome, grace, loue, maiestie.
In these sweet woods how often did you walke,
With Christ and his Apostles there to talke;
Placing his holy Writ in some faire tree,
To meditate what you therein did see:
With Moyses you did mount his holy Hill,
To know his pleasure, and performe his Will.
With louely Dauid did you often sing,
His holy Hymnes to Heauens Eternall King.
And in sweet musicke did your soule delight,
To sound his prayses, morning, noone, and night.
With blessed Ioseph you did often feed
Your pined brethren, when they stood in need.
And that sweet Lady sprung from Cliffords race,
Of noble Bedfords blood, faire steame [sic] of Grace;
To honourable Dorset now espows'd,
In whose faire breast true virtue then was hous'd:
Oh what delight did my weake spirits find,
In those pure parts of her well framed mind:
And yet it grieues me that I cannot be
Neere vnto her, whose virtues did agree
With those faire ornaments of outward beauty,
Which did enforce from all both loue and dutie.
Vnconstant Fortune, thou art most too blame,
Who casts vs downe into so lowe a frame:
Where our great friends wee cannot dayly see,

So great a diffrence is there in degree.
Many are placed in those Orbes of state,
Parters in honour, so ordain'd by Fate;
Neerer in show, yet farther off in loue,
In which, the lowest alwayes are aboue.
But whither am I carried in conceit?
My Wit too weake to conster of the great.
Why not? although we are but borne of earth,
We may behold the Heauens, despising death;
And louing heauen that is so farre aboue,
May in the end vouchsafe vs entire loue.
Therefore sweet Memorie doe thou retaine
Those pleasures past, which will not turne againe:
Remember beauteous Dorsets former sports,
So farre from beeing toucht by ill reports;
Wherein my selfe did alwaies beare a part,
While reuerend Loue presented my true heart:
Those recreations let me beare in mind,
Which her sweet youth and noble thoughts did finde:
Whereof depriu'd, I euermore must grieue,
Hating blind Fortune, carelesse to relieue.
And you sweet Cooke-ham, whom these Ladies leaue,
I now must tell the griefe you did conceaue
At their departure; when they went away,
How euery thing retaind a sad dismay:
Nay long before, when once an inkeling came,
Me thought each thing did vnto sorrow frame:
The trees that were so glorious in our view,
Forsooke both flowres and fruit, when once they knew,
Of your depart, their very leaues did wither,
Changing their colours as they grewe together.
But when they saw this had no powre to stay you,
They often wept, though speechlesse, could not pray you;
Letting their teares in your faire bosoms fall,
As if they said, Why will ye leaue vs all?
This beeing vaine, they cast their leaues away,
Hoping that pitie would haue made you stay:
Their frozen tops, like Ages hoarie haires,
Showes their disaster, languishing in feares:
A swarthy riueld ryne all ouer spread,
Their dying bodies half aliue, halfe dead.
But your occasions call'd you so away,
That nothing there had power to make you stay:
Yet did I see a noble gratefull minde,
Requiting each according to their kind,

Forgetting not to turne and take your leaue
Of these sad creatures, powrelesse to receiue
Your fauour, when with griefe you did depart,
Placing their former pleasures in your heart;
Giuing great charge to noble Memory,
There to preserue their loue continually:
But specially the loue of that faire tree,
That first and last you did vouchsafe to see:
In which it pleas'd you oft to take the ayre,
With noble Dorset, then a virgin faire:
Where many a learned Booke was read and skand
To this faire tree, taking me by the hand,
You did repeat the pleasures which had past,
Seeming to grieue they could no longer last.
And with a chaste, yet louing kisse tooke leaue,
Of which sweet kisse I did it soone bereaue:
Scorning a sencelesse creature should possesse
So rare a fauour, so great happinesse.
No other kisse it could receiue from me,
For feare to giue backe what it tooke of thee:
So I ingratefull Creature did deceiue it,
Of that which you vouchsaft in loue to leaue it.
And though it oft had giu'n me much content,
Yet this great wrong I neuer could repent:
But of the happiest made it most forlorne,
To shew that nothing's free from Fortunes scorne,
While all the rest with this most beauteous tree,
Made their sad consort Sorrowes harmony.
The Floures that on the banks and walkes did grow,
Crept in the ground, the Grasse did weepe for woe.
The Windes and Waters seem'd to chide togather,
Because you went away they knew not whither:
And those sweet Brookes that ranne so faire and cleare,
With griefe and trouble wrinckled did appeare.
Those preety Birds that wonted were to sing,
Now neither sing, nor chirp, nor vse their wing;
But with their tender feet on some bare spray,
Warble forth sorrow, and their owne dismay.
Faire Philomela leaues her mournefull Ditty,
Drownd in dead sleepe, yet can procure no pittie:
Each arbour, banke, each seate, each stately tree,
Lookes bare and desolate now for want of thee;
Turning greene tresses into frostie gray,
While in cold griefe they wither all away.
The Sunne grew weake, his beames no comfort gaue,

91

While all greene things did make the earth their graue:
Each brier, each bramble, when you went away,
Caught fast your clothes, thinking to make you stay:
Delightfull Eccho wonted to reply
To our last words, did now for sorrow die:
The house cast off each garment that might grace it,
Putting on Dust and Cobwebs to deface it.
All desolation then there did appeare,
When you were going whom they held so deare.
This last farewell to Cooke-ham here I giue,
When I am dead thy name in this may liue
Wherein I haue perform'd her noble hest,
Whose virtues lodge in my vnworthy breast,
And euer shall, so long as life remaines,
Tying my heart to her by those rich chaines.

SALVE DEUS REX JUDÆORUM.

Sith Cynthia is ascended to that rest
Of endlesse joy and true Eternitie,
That glorious place that cannot be exprest
By any wight clad in mortalitie,
In her almightie love so highly blest,
And crown'd with everlasting Sov'raigntie;
Where Saints and Angells do attend her Throne,
And she gives glorie unto God alone.
To thee great Countesse now I will applie
My Pen, to write thy never dying fame;
That when to Heav'n thy blessed Soule shall flie,.
These lines on earth record thy reverend name:
And to this taske I meane my Muse to tie,
Though wanting skill I shall but purchase blame:
Pardon (deere Ladie) want of womans wit
To pen thy praise, when few can equall it.
And pardon (Madame) though I do not write
Those praisefull lines of that delightfull place,

As you commaunded me in that faire night,
When shining Phoebe gave so great a grace,
Presenting Paradice to your sweet sight,
Unfolding all the beauty of her face
With pleasant groves, hills, walks and stately trees,
Which pleasures with retired minds agrees.

Whose Eagles eyes behold the glorious Sunne
Of th'all-creating Providence, reflecting
His blessed beames on all by him, begunne;
Increasing, strengthning, guiding and directing
All worldly creatures their due course to runne,
Unto His powrefull pleasure all subjecting:
And thou (deere Ladie) by his speciall grace,
In these his creatures dost behold his face.
Whose all-reviving beautie, yeelds such joyes
To thy sad Soule, plunged in waves of woe,
That worldly pleasures seemes to thee as toyes,
Onely thou seek'st Eternitie to know,
Respecting not the infinite annoyes
That Satan to thy well-staid mind can show;
Ne can he quench in thee, the Spirit of Grace,
Nor draw thee from beholding Heavens bright face.

Thy Mind so perfect by thy Maker fram'd,
No vaine delights can harbour in thy heart,
With his sweet love, thou art so much inflam'd,
As of the world thou seem'st to have no part;
So, love him still, thou need'st not be asham'd,
Tis He that made thee, what thou wert, and art:
Tis He that dries all teares from Orphans eies,
And heares from heav'n the wofull widdows cries.

Tis He that doth behold thy inward cares,
And will regard the sorrowes of thy Soule;
Tis He that guides thy feet from Sathans snares,
And in his Wisedome, doth thy waies controule:
He through afflictions, still thy Minde prepares,
And all thy glorious Trialls will enroule.
That when darke daies of terror shall appeare,
Thou as the Sunne shalt shine; or much more cleare.

The Heav'ns shall perish as a garment olde,
Or as a vesture by the maker chang'd,
And shall depart, as when a skrowle is rolde;
Yet thou from him shalt never be estrang'd,
When He shall come in glory, that was solde
For all our sinnes; we happily are chang'd,
Who for our faults put on his righteousnesse,
Although full oft his Lawes we doe transgresse.

Long mai'st thou joy in this almightie love,
Long may thy Soule be pleasing in his sight,
Long mai'st thou have true comforts from above,
Long mai'st thou set on him thy whole delight,
And patiently endure when he doth prove,
Knowing that He will surely do thee right:
Thy patience, faith, long suffring, and thy love,
He will reward with comforts from above.

With Majestie and Honour is He clad,
And deck'd with light, as with a garment faire;
He joyes the Meeke, and makes the Mightie sad,
Pulls downe the Prowd, and doth the Humble reare:
Who sees this Bridegroome, never can be sad;
None lives that can his wondrous workes declare:
Yea, looke how farre the Est is from the West,
So farre he sets our sinnes that have transgrest.

He rides upon the wings of all the windes,
And spreads the heav'ns with his all powrefull hand;
Oh! who can loose when the Almightie bindes?
Or in his angry presence dares to stand?
He searcheth out the secrets of all mindes;
All those that feare him, shall possesse the Land:
He is exceeding glorious to behold,
Antient of Times; so faire, and yet so old.

He of the watry Cloudes his Chariot frames,
And makes his blessed Angels powrefull Spirits
Rewarding all according to their merits;
The Righteous for an heritage he claimes,
And registers the wrongs of humble spirits:
Hills melt like wax, in presence of the Lord,
So do all sinners, in his sight abhorr'd.
He in the waters laies his chamber beames,
And cloudes of darkenesse compasse him about,
Consuming fire shall goe before in streames,
And burne up all his en'mies round about:
Yet on these Judgements worldlings never dreames,
Nor of these daungers never stand in doubt:
While he shall rest within his holy Hill,
That lives and dies according to his Will.
But woe to them that double-hearted bee,
Who with their tongues the righteous Soules doe slay;
Bending their bowes to shoot at all they see,

With upright hearts their Maker to obay;
And secretly doe let their arrowes flee,
To wound true hearted people any way:
The Lord wil roote them out that speake prowd things,
Deceitfull tongues are but false Slanders wings.

Froward are the ungodly from their berth,
No sooner borne, but they doe goe astray;
The Lord will roote them out from off the earth,
And give them to their en'mies for a pray,
As venemous as Serpents is their breath,
With poysned lies to hurt in what they may
The Innocent: who as a Dove shall flie
Unto the Lord, that he his cause may trie

The righteous Lord doth righteousnesse allow,
His countenance will behold the thing that's just;
Unto the Meane he makes the Mightie bow,
And raiseth up the Poore out of the dust:
Yet makes no count to us, nor when, nor how,
But powres his grace on all, that puts their trust
In him: that never will their hopes betray,
Nor lets them perish that for mercie pray.

He shall within his Tabernacle dwell,
Whose life is uncorrupt before the Lord,
Who no untrueths of Innocents doth tell,
Nor wrongs his neighbour, nor in deed, nor word,
Nor in his pride with malice seems to swell,
Nor whets his tongue more sharper than a sword,
To wound the reputation of the Just;
Nor seekes to lay their glorie in the Dust.

That great Jehova King of heav'n and earth,
Will raine downe fire and brimstone from above,
Upon the wicked monsters in their berth
That storme and rage at those whom he doth love:
Snares, stormes, and tempests he will raine,
and dearth,
Because he will himselfe almightie prove:
And this shall be their portion they shall drinke,
That thinkes the Lord is blind when he doth winke.

Pardon (good Madame) though I have digrest
From what I doe intend to write of thee,.
To set his glorie forth whom thou lov'st best,
Whose wondrous works no mortall eie can see;
His speciall care on those whom he hath blest
From wicked worldlings, how he sets them free:
And how such people he doth overthrow
In all their waies, that they his powre may know.

The meditation of this Monarchs love,
Drawes thee from caring what this world can yield;
Of joyes and griefes both equall thou dost prove,
They have no force, to force thee from the field:
Thy constant faith like to the Turtle Dove
Continues combat, and will never yield
To base affliction; or prowd pomps desire,
That sets the weakest mindes so much on fire.
Thou from the Court to the Countrie art retir'd,
Leaving the world, before the world leaves thee:
That great Enchantresse of weake mindes admir'd,
Whose all-bewitching charmes so pleasing be
To worldly wantons; and too much desir'd
Of those that care not for Eternitie:
But yeeld themselves as preys to Lust and Sinne,
Loosing their hopes of Heav'n Hell paines to winne.
But thou, the wonder of our wanton age
Leav'st all delights to serve a heav'nly King:
Who is more wise? or who can be more sage,
Than she that doth Affection subject bring;
Not forcing for the world, or Satans rage,
But shrowding under the Almighties wing;
Spending her yeares, moneths, daies,
minutes, howres,
In doing service to the heav'nly powres.
Thou faire example, live without compare,
With Honours triumphs seated in thy breast;
Pale Envy never can thy name empaire,
When in thy heart thou harbour'st such a guest:
Malice must live for ever in dispaire;
There's no revenge where Virtue still doth rest:
All hearts must needs do homage unto thee,
In whom all eies such rare perfection see.

That outward Beautie which the world commends,
Is not the subject I will write upon,
Whose date expir'd, that tyrant Time soone ends,
Those gawdie colours soone are spent and gone: unaccompanied
But those faire Virtues which on thee attends with virtue.
Are alwaies fresh, they never are but one:
They make thy Beautie fairer to behold,
Than was that Queenes for whom prowd Troy
was sold.

As for those matchlesse colours Red and White,
Or perfit features in a fading face,
Or due proportion pleasing to the sight;
All these doe draw but dangers and disgrace:
A mind enrich'd with Virtue, shines more bright,
Addes everlasting Beauty, gives true grace,
Frames an immortall Goddesse on the earth,
Who though she dies, yet Fame gives her new berth.

That pride of Nature which adornes the faire,
Like blasing Comets to allure all eies,
Is but the thred, that weaves their web of Care,
Who glories most, where most their danger lies;
For greatest perills do attend the faire,
When men do seeke, attempt, plot and devise,
How they may overthrow the chastest Dame,
Whose Beautie is the White whereat they aime.

Twas Beautie bred in Troy the ten yeares strife,
And carried Hellen from her lawfull Lord;
Twas Beautie made chaste Lucrece loose her life,
For which prowd Tarquins fact was so abhorr'd.
Beautie the cause Antonius wrong'd his wife,
Which could not be decided but by sword:
Great Cleopatraes Beautie and defects
Did worke Octaviaes wrongs, and his neglects.

What fruit did yeeld that faire forbidden tree,
But blood, dishonour, infamie, and shame?
Poore blinded Queene, could'st thou no better see,
But entertaine disgrace, in stead of fame?
Doe these designes with Majestie agree?
To staine thy blood, and blot thy royall name.
That heart that gave consent unto this ill,
Did give consent that thou thy selfe should'st kill.

Faire Rosamund, the wonder of her time,
Had bin much fairer, had shee not bin faire;
Beautie betraid her thoughts, aloft to clime,
To build strong castles in uncertaine aire,
Where th'infection of a wanton crime
Did worke her fall; first poyson, then despaire,
With double death did kill her perjur'd soule,
When heavenly Justice did her sinne controule.

Holy Matilda in a haplesse houre Of Matilda.
Was borne to sorow and to discontent,
Beauty the cause that turn'd her Sweet to Sowre,
While Chastity sought Folly to prevent.
Lustfull King John refus'd, did use his powre,
By Fire and Sword, to compasse his content:
But Friends disgrace, nor Fathers banishment,
Nor Death it selfe, could purchase her consent.

Here Beauty in the height of all perfection,
Crown'd this faire Creatures everlasting fame,
Whose noble minde did scorne the base subjection
Of Feares, or Favours, to impaire her Name:
By heavenly grace, she had such true direction,
To die with Honour, not to live in Shame;
And drinke that poyson with a cheerefull heart,
That could all Heavenly grace to her impart.

This Grace great Lady, doth possesse thy Soule,
And makes thee pleasing in thy Makers sight;
This Grace doth all imperfect Thoughts controule, the Introduction
Directing thee to serve thy God aright; to the passion
Still reckoning him, the Husband of thy Soule, of Christ.
Which is most pretious in his glorious sight:
Because the Worlds delights shee doth denie
For him, who for her sake vouchsaf'd to die.

And dying made her Dowager of all;
Nay more, Co-heire of that eternall blisse
That Angels lost, and We by Adams fall;
Meere Cast-awaies, rais'd by a Judas kisse,
Christs bloody sweat, the Vineger, and Gall,
The Speare, Sponge, Nailes, his buffeting with Fists,
His bitter Passion, Agony, and Death,
Did gaine us Heaven when He did loose his breath.

These high deserts invites my lowely Muse
To write of Him, and pardon crave of thee,
For Time so spent, I need make no excuse, before
Knowing it doth with thy faire Minde agree the Passion.
So well, as thou no Labour wilt refuse,
That to thy holy Love may pleasing be:

His Death and Passion I desire to write,
And thee to reade, the blessed Soules delight.
But my deare Muse, now whither wouldst thou flie,
Above the pitch of thy appointed straine?
With Icarus thou seekest now to trie,
Not waxen wings, but thy poore barren Braine,
Which farre too weake, these siely lines descrie;
Yet cannot this thy forward Mind restraine,
But thy poore Infant Verse must soare aloft,
Not fearing threat'ning dangers, happening oft.

Thinke when the eye of Wisdom shall discover
Thy weakling Muse to flie, that scarce could creepe,
And in the Ayre above the Clowdes to hover,
When better 'twere mued up, and fast asleepe;
They'l thinke with Phaeton, thou canst neare recover,
But helplesse with that poore yong Lad to weepe:
The little World of thy weake Wit on fire,
Where thou wilt perish in thine owne desire.

But yet the Weaker thou doest seeme to be
In Sexe, or Sence, the more his Glory shines,
That doth infuze such powerfull Grace in thee,
To shew thy Love in these few humble Lines;
The Widowes Myte, with this may well agree,
Her little All more worth than golden mynes,
Beeing more deerer to our loving Lord,
Than all the wealth that Kingdoms could affoard.

Therefore I humbly for his Grace will pray,
That he will give me Power and Strength to Write,
That what I have begun, so end I may,
As his great Glory may appeare more bright;
Yea in these Lines I may no further stray,
Than his most holy Spirit shall give me Light:
That blindest Weakenesse be not over-bold,
The manner of his Passion to unfold.

In other Phrases than may well agree
With his pure Doctrine, and most holy Writ,
That Heavens cleare eye, and all the World may see,
I seeke his Glory, rather than to get
The Vulgars breath, the seed of Vanitie,
Nor Fames lowd Trumpet care I to admit;
But rather strive in plainest Words to showe,
The Matter which I seeke to undergoe.

A Matter farre beyond my barren skill,
To shew with any Life this map of Death,
This Storie; that whole Worlds with Bookes would fill,
In these few Lines, will put me out of breath,
To run so swiftly up this mightie Hill,
I may behold it with the eye of Faith;
But to present this pure unspotted Lambe,
I must confesse, I farre unworthy am.

Yet if he please t'illuminate my Spirit,
And give me Wisdom from his holy Hill,
That I may Write part of his glorious Merit,
If he vouchsafe to guide my Hand and Quill,
To shew his Death, by which we doe inherit
Those endlesse Joyes that all our hearts doe fill;
Then will I tell of that sad blacke fac'd Night,
Whose mourning Mantle covered Heavenly Light.

That very Night our Saviour was betrayed, Here begins
Oh night! exceeding all the nights of sorow
When our most blessed Lord, although dismayed,.
Yet would not he one Minutes respite borrow,
But to Mount Olives went, though sore afraid,
To welcome Night, and entertaine the Morrow;
And as he oft unto that place did goe,
So did he now, to meete his long nurst woe.

He told his deere Disciples that they all
Should be offended by him, that selfe night,
His Griefe was great, and theirs could not be small,
To part from him who was their sole Delight;
Saint Peter thought his Faith could never fall,
No mote could happen in so cleare a sight:
Which made him say, though all men
were offended,
Yet would he never, though his life were ended.

But his deare Lord made answere, That before
The Cocke did crowe, he should deny him thrice;
This could not choose but grieve him very sore,
That his hot Love should proove more cold than Ice,
Denying him he did so much adore;
No imperfection in himselfe he spies,
But faith againe, with him hee'l surely die,
Rather than his deare Master once denie.

And all the rest (did likewise say the same)
Of his Disciples, at that instant time;
But yet poore Peter, he was most too blame,
That thought above them all, by Faith to clime;
His forward speech inflicted sinne and shame,
When Wisdoms eyes did looke and checke his crime:
Who did foresee, and told it him before,
Yet would he needs averre it more and more.

Now went our Lord unto that holy place,
Sweet Gethsemaine hallowed by his presence,
That blessed Garden, which did now embrace
His holy corps, yet could make no defence
Against those Vipers, objects of disgrace,
Which sought that pure eternall Love to quench:
Here his Disciples willed he to stay,
Whilst he went further, where he meant to pray.

None were admitted with their Lord to goe,
But Peter, and the sonnes of Zebed'us,
To them good Jesus opened all his woe,
He gave them leave his sorows to discusse,
His deepest griefes, he did not scorne to showe
These three deere friends, so much he did intrust:
Beeing sorowfull, and overcharg'd with griefe,
He told it them, yet look'd for no reliefe.

Sweet Lord, how couldst thou thus to flesh and blood
Communicate thy griefe? tell of thy woes?
Thou knew'st they had no powre to doe thee good,
But were the cause thou must endure these blowes,
Beeing the Scorpions bred in Adams mud,
Whose poys'ned sinnes did worke among thy foes,
To re-ore-charge thy over-burd'ned soule,
Although the sorowes now they doe condole.
Yet didst thou tell them of thy troubled state,

101

Of thy Soules heavinesse unto the death,
So full of Love, so free wert thou from hate,
To bid them stay, whose sinnes did stop thy breath,
When thou wert entring at so straite a gate,
Yea entring even into the doore of Death,
Thou bidst them tarry there, and watch with thee,
Who from thy pretious blood-shed were not free.

Bidding them tarry, thou didst further goe,
To meet affliction in such gracefull sort,
As might moove pitie both in friend and foe,
Thy sorowes such, as none could them comport,
Such great Indurements who did ever know,
When to th' Almighty thou didst make resort?
And falling on thy face didst humbly pray,
If 'twere his Will that Cup might passe away.

Saying, Not my will, but thy will Lord be done.
When as thou prayedst an Angel did appeare
From Heaven, to comfort thee Gods onely Sonne,
That thou thy Suffrings might'st the better beare, Beeing in an agony, thy glasse neere run,
Thou prayedst more earnestly, in so great feare,
That pretious sweat came trickling to the ground,
Like drops of blood thy sences to confound.

Loe here his Will, not thy Will, Lord was done,
And thou content to undergoe all paines,
Sweet Lambe of God, his deare beloved Sonne,
By this great purchase, what to thee remaines?
Of Heaven and Earth thou hast a Kingdom wonne,
Thy Glory beeing equall with thy Gaines,
In ratifying Gods promise on the Earth,
Made many hundred yeares before thy birth.

But now returning to thy sleeping Friends,
That could not watch one houre for love of thee,
Even those three Friends, which on thy Grace depends,
Yet shut those Eies that should their Maker see;
What colour, what excuse, or what amends,
From thy Displeasure now can set them free?
Yet thy pure Pietie bids them Watch and Pray,
Lest in Temptation they be led away.
Although the Spirit was willing to obay,
Yet what great weakenesse in the Flesh was found!

102

They slept in Ease, whilst thou in Paine didst pray;
Loe, they in Sleepe, and thou in Sorow drown'd:
Yet Gods right Hand was unto thee a stay,
When horror, griefe, and sorow did abound:
His Angel did appeare from Heaven to thee,
To yeeld thee comfort in Extremitie.

But what could comfort then thy troubled Minde,
When Heaven and Earth were both against thee bent?
And thou no hope, no ease, no rest could'st finde,
But must restore that Life, which was but lent;
Was ever Creature in the World so kinde,
But he that from Eternitie was sent?
To satisfie for many Worlds of Sinne,
Whose matchlesse Torments did but then begin.

If one Mans sinne doth challendge Death and Hell,
With all the Torments that belong thereto:
If for one sinne such Plagues on David fell,
As grieved him, and did his Seed undoe:
If Salomon, for that he did not well,
Falling from Grace, did loose his Kingdome too:
Ten Tribes beeing taken from his wilfull Sonne
And Sinne the Cause that they were all undone.
What could thy Innocency now expect,
When all the Sinnes that ever were committed,
Were laid to thee, whom no man could detect?
Yet farre thou wert of Man from beeing pittied,
The Judge so just could yeeld thee no respect,
Nor would one jot of penance be remitted;
But greater horror to thy Soule must rise,
Than Heart can thinke, or any Wit devise.

Now drawes the houre of thy affliction neere,
And ugly Death presents himselfe before thee;
Thou now must leave those Friends thou held'st so deere,
Yea those Disciples, who did most adore thee;
Yet in thy countenance doth no Wrath appeare,
Although betrayd to those that did abhorre thee:
Thou did'st vouchsafe to visit them againe,
Who had no apprehension of thy paine.
Their eyes were heavie, and their hearts asleepe,
Nor knew they well what answere then to make thee;
Yet thou as Watchman, had'st a care to keepe
Those few from sinne, that shortly would forsake thee;

But now thou bidst them henceforth Rest and Sleepe,
Thy houre is come, and they at hand to take thee:
The Sonne of God to Sinners made a pray,
Oh hatefull houre! oh blest! oh cursed day!

Loe here thy great Humility was found,
Beeing King of Heaven, and Monarch of the Earth,
Yet well content to have thy Glory drownd,
By beeing counted of so meane a berth;
Grace, Love, and Mercy did so much abound,
Thou entertaindst the Crosse, even to the death:
And nam'dst thy selfe, the sonne of Man to be,
To purge our pride by thy Humilitie.

But now thy friends whom thou didst call to goe,
Heavy Spectators of thy haplesse case,
See thy Betrayer, whom too well they knowe,
One of the twelve, now object of disgrace,
A trothlesse traytor, and a mortall foe,
With fained kindnesse seekes thee to imbrace;
And gives a kisse, whereby he may deceive thee,
That in the hands of Sinners he might leave thee.

Now muster forth with Swords, with Staves, with Bils,
High Priests and Scribes, and Elders of the Land,
Seeking by force to have their wicked Wils,
Which thou didst never purpose to withstand;
Now thou mak'st haste unto the worst of Ils,
And who they seeke, thou gently doest demand;
This didst thou Lord, t'amaze these Fooles the more,
T'inquire of that, thou knew'st so well before.

When loe these Monsters did not shame to tell,
His name they sought, and found, yet could not know
Jesus of Nazareth, at whose feet they fell,
When Heavenly Wisdome did descend so lowe
To speake to them: they knew they did not well,
Their great amazement made them backeward goe:
Nay, though he said unto them, I am he,
They could not know him, whom their eyes did see.

How blinde were they could not discerne the Light!
How dull! if not to understand the truth,
How weake! if meekenesse overcame their might;
How stony hearted, if not mov'd to ruth:

How void of Pitie, and how full of Spight,
Gainst him that was the Lord of Light and Truth:
Here insolent Boldnesse checkt by Love and Grace,
Retires, and falls before our Makers face.

For when he spake to this accursed crew,
And mildely made them know that it was he:
Presents himselfe, that they might take a view;
And what they doubted they might cleerely see;
Nay more, to re-assure that it was true,
He said: I say unto you, I am hee.
If him they sought, he's willing to obay,
Onely desires the rest might goe their way.

Thus with a heart prepared to endure
The greatest wrongs Impietie could devise,
He was content to stoope unto their Lure,
Although his Greatnesse might doe otherwise:
Here Grace was seised on with hands impure,
And Virtue now must be supprest by Vice,
Pure Innocencie made a prey to Sinne,
Thus did his Torments and our Joyes beginne.

Here faire Obedience shined in his breast,
And did suppresse all feare of future paine;
Love was his Leader unto this unrest,
Whil'st Righteousnesse doth carry up his Traine;
Mercy made way to make us highly blest,
When Patience beat downe Sorrow, Feare and Paine:
Justice sate looking with an angry brow,
On blessed misery appeering now.

More glorious than all the Conquerors
Than ever liv'd within this Earthly round,
More powrefull than all Kings, or Governours
That ever yet within this World were found;
More valiant than the greatest Souldiers
That ever fought, to have their glory crown'd:
For which of them, that ever yet tooke breath,
Sought t'indure the doome of Heaven and Earth?

But our sweet Saviour whom these Jewes did name;
Yet could their learned Ignorance apprehend
No light of grace, to free themselves from blame:
Zeale, Lawes, Religion, now they doe pretend
Against the truth, untruths they seeke to frame:
Now al their powres, their wits, their strengths,
they bend
Against one siely, weake, unarmed man,
Who no resistance makes, though much he can,
To free himselfe from these unlearned men,
Who call'd him Saviour in his blessed name;
Yet farre from knowing him their Saviour then,
That came to save both them and theirs from blame;
Though they retire and fall, they come agen
To make a surer purchase of their shame:
With lights and torches now they find the way,
To take the Shepheard whilst the sheep doe stray.

Why should unlawfull actions use the Light?
Inniquitie in Darkenesse seekes to dwell;
Sinne rides his circuit in the dead of Night,
Teaching all soules the ready waies to hell;
Sathan coms arm'd with all the powres of Spight,
Heartens his Champions, makes them rude and fell;
Like rav'ning wolves, to shed his guiltlesse blood,
Who thought no harme, but di'd to doe them good.

Here Falshood beares the shew of formall Right,
Base Treacherie hath gote a guard of men;
Tyranny attends, with all his strength and might,
To leade this siely Lamb to Lyons denne;
Yet he unmoov'd in this most wretched plight,
Goes on to meete them, knowes the houre, and when:
The powre of darkenesse must expresse Gods ire,
Therefore to save these few was his desire.
These few that wait on Poverty and Shame,
And offer to be sharers in his Ils;
These few that will be spreaders of his Fame,
He will not leave to Tyrants wicked wils
But still desires to free them from all blame,
Yet Feare goes forward, Anger Patience kils:
A Saint is mooved to revenge a wrong,
And Mildnesse doth what doth to Wrath belong.

For Peter griev'd at what might then befall,
Yet knew not what to doe, nor what to thinke,
Thought something must be done; now, if at all,
To free his Master, that he might not drinke
This poys'ned draught, farre bitterer than gall,
For now he sees him at the very brinke
Of griesly Death, who gins to shew his face,
Clad in all colours of a deepe disgrace.

And now those hands, that never us'd to fight,
Or drawe a weapon in his owne defence,
Too forward is, to doe his Master right,
Since of his wrongs, hee feeles so true a sence:
But ah poore Peter! now thou wantest might,
And hee's resolv'd, with them he will goe hence:
To draw thy sword in such a helpelesse cause,
Offends thy Lord, and is against the Lawes.

So much he hates Revenge, so farre from Hate,
That he vouchsafes to heale, whom thou dost wound;
His paths are Peace, with none he holdes Debate,
His Patience stands upon so sure a ground,
To counsell thee, although it comes too late:
Nay, to his foes, his mercies so abound,
That he in pitty doth thy will restraine,
And heales the hurt, and takes away the paine.

For willingly he will endure this wrong,
Although his pray'rs might have obtain'd such grace,
As to dissolve their plots though ne'r so strong,
And bring these wicked Actors in worse case
Than Ægypts King on whom Gods plagues did throng,
But that foregoing Sculptures must take place:
If God by prayers had an army sent
Of powrefull Angels, who could them prevent?

Yet mightie JESUS meekely ask'd, Why they
With Swords and Staves doe come as to a Thiefe?
Hee teaching in the Temple day by day
None did offend, or give him cause of griefe.
Now all are forward, glad is he that may
Give most offence, and yeeld him least reliefe:
His hatefull foes are ready now to take him,
And all his deere Disciples do forsake him.

Those deare Disciples that he most did love,
And were attendant at his becke and call,
When triall of affliction came to prove,
They first left him, who now must leave them all:
For they were earth, and he came from above,
Which made them apt to flie, and fit to fall:
Though they protest they never will forsake him,
They do like men, when dangers overtake them.

And he alone is bound to loose us all,
Whom with unhallowed hands they led along,
To wicked Caiphas in the Judgement Hall,
Who studies onely how to doe him wrong;
High Priests and Elders, People great and small,
With all reprochfull words about him throng:
False Witnesses are now call'd in apace,
Whose trothlesse tongues must make pale
death imbrace

The beauty of the World, Heavens chiefest Glory;
The mirrour of Martyrs, Crowne of holy Saints;
Love of th'Almighty, blessed Angels story;
Water of Life, which none that drinks it, faints;
Guide of the Just, where all our Light we borrow;
Mercy of Mercies; Hearer of Complaints;
Triumpher over Death; Ransomer of Sinne;
Falsly accused: now his paines begin.
Their tongues doe serve him as a Passing bell,
For what they say is certainly beleeved;
So sound a tale unto the Judge they tell,
That he of Life must shortly be bereaved;
Their share of Heaven, they doe not care to sell,
So his afflicted Heart be throughly grieved:
They tell his Words, though farre from his intent,
And what his Speeches were, not what he meant.
That he Gods holy Temple could destroy,
And in three daies could build it up againe;
This seem'd to them a vaine and idle toy,
It would not sinke into their sinful braine:
Christs blessed body, al true Christians joy,
Should die, and in three dayes revive againe:
This did the Lord of Heaven and earth endure,
Unjustly to be charg'd by tongues impure.

108

And now they all doe give attentive eare,
To heare the answere, which he will not make;
The people wonder how he can forbeare,
And these great wrongs so patiently can take;
But yet he answers not, nor doth he care,
Much more he will endure for our sake:
Nor can their wisdoms any way discover,
Who he should be that proov'd so true a Lover.
To entertaine the sharpest pangs of death,
And fight a combate in the depth of hell,
For wretched Worldlings made of dust and earth,
Whose hard'ned hearts, with pride and mallice swell;
In midst of bloody sweat, and dying breath,
He had compassion on these tyrants fell:

And purchast them a place in Heav'n for ever,
When they his Soule and Body sought to sever.
Sinnes ugly mists, so blinded had their eyes,
That at Noone dayes they could discerne no Light;
These were those fooles, that thought themselves so wise,
The Jewish wolves, that did our Saviour bite;
For now they use all meanes they can devise,
To beate downe truth, and goe against all right:
Yea now they take Gods holy name in vaine,
To know the truth, which truth they doe prophane.

The chiefest Hel-hounds of this hatefull crew,
Rose up to aske what answere he could make,
Against those false accusers in his view;
That by his speech, they might advantage take:
He held his peace, yet knew they said not true,
No answere would his holy wisdome make,
Till he was charged in his glorious name,
Whose pleasure 'twas he should endure this shame.

Then with so mild a Majestie he spake,
As they might easily know from whence he came,
His harmelesse tongue doth no exceptions take,
Nor Priests, nor People, meanes he now to blame;
But answers Folly, for true Wisdomes sake,
Beeing charged deeply by his powrefull name,
To tell if Christ the Sonne of God he be,
Who for our sinnes must die, to set us free.
To thee O Caiphas doth he answere give,
That thou hast said, what thou desir'st to know,

And yet thy malice will not let him live,
So much thou art unto thy selfe a foe;
He speaketh truth, but thou wilt not beleeve,
Nor canst thou apprehend it to be so:
Though he expresse his Glory unto thee,
Thy Owly eies are blind, and cannot see.

Thou rend'st thy° cloathes, in stead of thy false heart,
And on the guiltlesse lai'st thy guilty crime;
For thou blasphem'st, and he must feele the smart:
To sentence death, thou think'st it now high time;
No witnesse now thou need'st, for this fowle part,
Thou to the height of wickednesse canst clime:
And give occasion to the ruder sort,
To make afflictions, sorrows, follies sport.

Now when the dawne of day gins to appeare,
And all your wicked counsels have an end,
To end his Life, that holds you all so deere,
For to that purpose did your studies bend;
Proud Pontius Pilate must the matter heare,
To your untroths his eares he now must lend:
Sweet Jesus bound, to him you led away,
Of his most pretious blood to make your pray.

Which, when that wicked Caytife did perceive,
By whose lewd meanes he came to this distresse;
He brought the price of blood he did receive,
Thinking thereby to make his fault seeme lesse,
And with these Priests and Elders did it leave,
Confest his fault, wherein he did transgresse:
But when he saw Repentance unrespected,
He hang'd himselfe; of God and Man rejected.

By this Example, what can be expected
From wicked Man, which on the Earth doth live?
But faithlesse dealing, feare of God neglected;
Who for their private gaine cares not to sell
The Innocent Blood of Gods most deere elected,
As did that caytife wretch, now damn'd in Hell:
If in Christs Schoole, he tooke so great a fall,
What will they doe, that come not there at all.
Now Pontius Pilate is to judge the Cause
Of faultlesse Jesus, who before him stands;

Who neither hath offended Prince, nor Lawes,
Although he now be brought in woefull bands:
O noble Governour, make thou yet a pause,
Doe not in innocent blood imbrue thy hands;
But heare the words of thy most worthy wife,
Who sends to thee, to beg her Saviours life.

Let barb'rous crueltie farre depart from thee,
And in true Justice take afflictions part;
Open thine eies, that thou the truth mai'st see,
Doe not the thing that goes against thy heart,
Condemne not him that must thy Saviour be;
But view his holy Life, his good desert.
Let not us Women glory in Mens fall,
Who had power given to over-rule us all.

Till now your indiscretion sets us free, *Eves Apologie.*
And makes our former fault much lesse appeare;
Our Mother Eve, who tasted of the Tree,
Giving to Adam what shee held most deare,
Was simply good, and had no powre to see,
The after-comming harme did not appeare:
The subtile Serpent that our Sex betraide,
Before our fall so sure a plot had laide.

That undiscerning Ignorance perceav'd
No guile, or craft that was by him intended;
For had she knowne, of what we were bereav'd,
To his request she had not condiscended.
But she (poore soule) by cunning was deceav'd,
No hurt therein her harmelesse Heart intended:
For she alleadg'd Gods word, which he denies,
That they should die, but even as Gods, be wise.

But surely Adam can not be excusde,
Her fault though great, yet hee was most too blame;
What Weaknesse offerd, Strength might have refusde,
Being Lord of all, the greater was his shame:
Although the Serpents craft had her abusde,
Gods holy word ought all his actions frame,
For he was Lord and King of all the earth,
Before poore Eve had either life or breath.

Who being fram'd by Gods eternall hand,
The perfect'st man that ever breath'd on earth;
And from Gods mouth receiv'd that strait command,
The breach whereof he knew was present death:
Yea having powre to rule both Sea and Land,
Yet with one Apple wonne to loose that breath
Which God had breathed in his beauteous face,
Bringing us all in danger and disgrace.

And then to lay the fault on Patience backe,
That we (poore women) must endure it all;
We know right well he did discretion lacke,
Beeing not perswaded thereunto at all;
If Eve did erre, it was for knowledge sake,
The fruit beeing faire perswaded him to fall:
No subtill Serpents falshood did betray him,
If he would eate it, who had powre to stay him?
Not Eve, whose fault was onely too much love,
Which made her give this present to her Deare,
That what shee tasted, he likewise might prove,
Whereby his knowledge might become more cleare;
He never sought her weakenesse to reprove,
With those sharpe words, which he of God did heare:
Yet Men will boast of Knowledge, which he tooke
From Eves faire hand, as from a learned Booke.

If any Evill did in her remaine,
Beeing made of him, he was the ground of all;
If one of many Worlds could lay a staine
Upon our Sexe, and worke so great a fall
To wretched Man, by Satans subtill traine;
What will so fowle a fault amongst you all?
Her weakenesse did the Serpents words obay;
But you in malice Gods deare Sonne betray.

Whom, if unjustly you condemne to die,
Her sinne was small, to what you doe commit;
All mortall sinnes that doe for vengeance crie,
Are not to be compared unto it:
If many worlds would altogether trie,
By all their sinnes the wrath of God to get;
This sinne of yours, surmounts them all as farre
As doth the Sunne, another little starre,

Then let us have our Libertie againe,
And challendge to your selves no Sov'raigntie;
You came not in the world without our paine,
Make that a barre against your crueltie;
Your fault beeing greater, why should you disdaine
Our beeing your equals, free from tyranny?
If one weake woman simply did offend,
This sinne of yours, hath no excuse, nor end.

To which (poore soules) we never gave consent,
Witnesse thy wife (O Pilate) speakes for all;
Who did but dreame, and yet a message sent,
That thou should'st have nothing to doe at all
With that just man; which, if thy heart relent,
Why wilt thou be a reprobate with Saul?
To seeke the death of him that is so good,
For thy soules health to shed his dearest blood.

Yea, so thou mai'st these sinful people please,
Thou art content against all truth and right,
To seale this act, that may procure thine ease
With blood, and wrong, with tyrannie, and might;
The multitude thou seekest to appease,
By base dejection of this heavenly Light:
Demanding which of these that thou should'st loose,
Whether the Thiefe, or Christ King of the Jewes.
Base Barrabas the Thiefe, they all desire,
And thou more base than he, perform'st their will;
Yet when thy thoughts backe to themselves retire,
Thou art unwilling to commit this ill:
Oh that thou couldst unto such grace aspire,
That thy polluted lips might never kill
That Honour, which right Judgement ever graceth,
To purchase shame, which all true worth defaceth.

Art thou a Judge, and asketh what to do
With one, in whom no fault there can be found?
The death of Christ wilt thou consent unto,
Finding no cause, no reason, nor no ground?
Shall he be scourg'd, and crucified too?
And must his miseries by thy meanes abound?
Yet not asham'd to aske what he hath done,
When thine owne conscience seeks this sinne
to shunne.

113

Three times thou ask'st, What evill hath he done?
And saist, thou find'st in him no cause of death,
Yet wilt thou chasten Gods beloved Sonne,
Although to thee no word of ill he saith:
For Wrath must end, what Malice hath begunne,
And thou must yield to stop his guiltlesse breath.
This rude tumultuous rowt doth presse so sore,
That thou condemnest him thou shouldst adore.

Yet Pilate, this can yeeld thee no content,
To exercise thine owne authoritie,
But unto Herod he must needes be sent,
To reconcile thy selfe by tyrannie:
Was this the greatest good in Justice meant,
When thou perceiv'st no fault in him to be?
If thou must make thy peace by Virtues fall,
Much better 'twere not to be friends at all.

Yet neither thy sterne browe, nor his great place,
Can draw an answer from the Holy One:
His false accusers, nor his great disgrace,
Nor Herods scoffes; to him they are all one:
He neither cares, nor feares his owne ill case,
Though being despis'd and mockt of every one:
King Herods gladnesse gives him little ease,
Neither his anger seekes he to appease.

Yet this is strange, that base Impietie
Should yeeld those robes of honour, which were due;
Pure white, to shew his great Integritie,
His innocency, that all the world might view;
Perfections height in lowest penury,
Such glorious poverty as they never knew:
Purple and Scarlet well might him beseeme,
Whose pretious blood must all the world redeeme.

And that Imperiall Crowne of Thornes he wore,
Was much more pretious than the Diadem
Of any King that ever liv'd before,
Or since his time, their honour's but a dreame
To his eternall glory, beeing so poore,
To make a purchasse of that heavenly Realme;
Where God with all his Angels lives in peace,
No griefes, nor sorrowes, but all joyes increase.

Those royall robes, which they in scorne did give,
To make him odious to the common sort,
Yeeld light of Grace to those whose soules shall live
Within the harbour of this heavenly port;
Much doe they joy, and much more doe they grieve,
His death, their life, should make his foes such sport:
With sharpest thornes to pricke his blessed face,
Our joyfull sorrow, and his greater grace.

Three feares at once possessed Pilates heart;
The first, Christs innocencie, which so plaine appeares;
The next, That he which now must feele this smart,
Is Gods deare Sonne, for any thing he heares:
But that which proov'd the deepest wounding dart,
Is Peoples threat'nings, which he so much feares,
That he to Cæsar could not be a friend,
Unlesse he sent sweet JESUS to his end.

Now Pilate thou art proov'd a painted wall,
A golden Sepulcher with rotten bones;
From right to wrong, from equitie to fall:
If none upbraid thee, yet the very stones
His blood, his teares, his sighes, his bitter groanes:
All these will witnesse at the latter day,
When water cannot wash thy sinne away.

Canst thou be innocent, that gainst all right,
Wilt yeeld to what thy conscience doth withstand?
Beeing a man of knowledge, powre, and might,
To let the wicked carrie such a hand,
Before thy face to blindfold Heav'ns bright light,
And thou to yeeld to what they did demand?
Washing thy hands, thy conscience cannot cleare,
But to all worlds this staine must needs appeare.

For loe, the Guiltie doth accuse the Just,
And faultie Judge condemnes the Innocent;
And wilfull Jewes to exercise their lust,
With whips and taunts against their Lord are bent;
He basely us'd, blasphemed, scorn'd, and curst,
Our heavenly King to death for us they sent:
Reproches, slanders, spittings in his face,
Spight doing all her worst in his disgrace.

And now this long expected houre drawes neere,
When blessed Saints with Angels doe condole;
His holy march, soft pace, and heavy cheere,
In humble sort to yeeld his glorious soule,
By his deserts the fowlest sinnes to cleare;
And in th'eternall booke of heaven to enroule
A satisfaction till the generall doome,
Of all sinnes past, and all that are to come.

They that had seene this pitifull Procession,
From Pilates Palace to Mount Calvarie,
Might thinke he answer'd for some great transgression,
Beeing in such odious sort condemn'd to die;
He plainely shewed that his own profession
Was virtue, patience, grace, love, piety;
And how by suffering he could conquer more
Than all the Kings that ever liv'd before.

First went the Crier with open mouth proclayming
The heavy sentence of Iniquitie,
The Hangman next, by his base office clayming
His right in Hell, where sinners never die,
Carrying the nayles, the people still blaspheming
Their maker, using all impiety;
The Thieves attending him on either side,
The Serjeants watching, while the women cri'd. The teares
of the
Thrice happy women that obtaind such grace daughters
From him whose worth the world could not containe.
Immediately to turne about his face,
As not remembring his great griefe and paine,
To comfort you, whose teares powr'd forth apace
On Flora's bankes, like shewers of Aprils raine:
Your cries inforced mercie, grace, and love
From him, whom greatest Princes could not moove:

To speake on word, nor once to lift his eyes
Unto proud Pilate, no nor Herod, king;
By all the Questions that they could devise,
Could make him answere to no manner of thing;
Yet these poore women, by their pitious cries
Did moove their Lord, their Lover, and their King,
To take compassion, turne about, and speake
To them whose hearts were ready now to breake.

116

Most blessed daughters of Jerusalem,
Who found such favour in your Saviors sight,
To turne his face when you did pitie him;
Your tearefull eyes, beheld his eies more bright;
Your Faith and Love unto such grace did clime,
To have reflection from this Heav'nly Light:
Your Eagles eyes did gaze against this Sunne,
Your hearts did thinke, he dead, the world were done.
When spightfull men with torments did oppresse
Th'afflicted body of this innocent Dove,
Poore women seeing how much they did transgresse,
By teares, by sighes, by cries intreat,
What may be done among the thickest presse,
They labour still these tyrants hearts to move;
In pitie and compassion to forbeare
Their whipping, spurning, tearing of his haire.

But all in vaine, their malice hath no end,
Their hearts more hard than flint, or marble stone;
Now to his griefe, his greatnesse they attend,
When he (God knowes) had rather be alone;
They are his guard, yet seeke all meanes to offend:
Well may he grieve, well may he sigh and groane,
Under the burthen of a heavy crosse,
He faintly goes to make their gaine his losse.

His woefull Mother wayting on her Sonne,
All comfortlesse in depth of sorow drowned;
Her griefes extreame, although but new begun,
To see his bleeding body oft shee swouned;
How could shee choose but thinke her selfe undone,
He dying, with whose glory shee was crowned?
None ever lost so great a losse as shee,
Beeing Sonne, and Father of Eternitie.

Her teares did wash away his pretious blood,
That sinners might not tread it under feet
To worship him, and that it did her good
Upon her knees, although in open street,
Knowing he was the Jessie floure and bud,
That must be gath'red when it smell'd most sweet:
Her Sonne, her Husband, Father, Saviour, King,
Whose death killd Death, and tooke away his sting.

Most blessed Virgin, in whose faultlesse fruit,
All Nations of the earth must needes rejoyce,
No Creature having sence though ne'r so brute,
But joyes and trembles when they heare his voyce;
His wisedome strikes the wisest persons mute,
Faire chosen vessell, happy in his choyce:
Deere Mother of our Lord, whose reverend name,
All people Blessed call, and spread thy fame.

For the Almightie magnified thee,
And looked downe upon thy meane estate;
Thy lowly mind, and unstain'd Chastitie
Did pleade for Love at great Jehovaes gate,
Who sending swift-wing'd Gabriel unto thee,
His holy will and pleasure to relate;
To thee most beauteous Queene of Woman-kind,
The Angell did unfold his Makers mind.
He thus beganne, Haile Mary full of grace,
Thou freely art beloved of the Lord, of the Virgin
He is with thee, behold thy happy case; Marie.
What endlesse comfort did these words afford
To thee that saw'st an Angell in the place
Proclaime thy Virtues worth, and to record
Thee blessed among women: that thy praise
Should last so many worlds beyond thy daies.

Loe, this high message to thy troubled spirit,
He doth deliver in the plainest sence;
Sayes, Thou shouldst beare a Sonne that shal inherit
His Father Davids throne, free from offence,
Call's him that Holy thing, by whose pure merit
We must be sav'd, tels what he is, of whence;
His worth, his greatnesse, what his name must be,
Who should be call'd the Sonne of the most High.

He cheeres thy troubled soule, bids thee not feare;
When thy pure thoughts could hardly apprehend
This salutation, when he did appeare;
Nor couldst thou judge, whereto those words
did tend;
His pure aspect did moove thy modest cheere
To muse, yet joy that God vouchsaf'd to send
His glorious Angel; who did thee assure
To beare a child, although a Virgin pure.

Nay more, thy Sonne should Rule and Raigne
for ever;
Yea, of his Kingdom there should be no end;
Over the house of Jacob, Heavens great Giver
Would give him powre, and to that end did send
His faithfull servant Gabriel to deliver
To thy chast eares no word that might offend:
But that this blessed Infant borne of thee,
Thy Sonne, The onely Sonne of God should be.
When on the knees of thy submissive heart
Thou humbly didst demand, How that should be?
Thy virgin thoughts did thinke, none could impart
This great good hap, and blessing unto thee;
Farre from desire of any man thou art,
Knowing not one, thou art from all men free:
When he, to answere this thy chaste desire,
Gives thee more cause to wonder and admire.

That thou a blessed Virgin shoulst remaine,
Yea that the holy Ghost should come on thee
A maiden Mother, subject to no paine,
For highest powre should overshadow thee:
Could thy faire eyes from teares of joy refraine,
When God look'd downe upon thy poore degree?
Making thee Servant, Mother, Wife, and Nurse
To Heavens bright King, that freed us from the curse.
Thus beeing crown'd with glory from above,
Grace and Perfection resting in thy breast,
Thy humble answer doth approve thy Love,
And all these sayings in thy heart doe rest:
Thy Child a Lambe, and thou a Turtle dove,
Above all other women highly blest;
To find such favour in his glorious sight,
In whom thy heart and soule doe most delight.

What wonder in the world more strange could seeme,
Than that a Virgin could conceive and beare
Within her wombe a Sonne, That should redeeme
All Nations on the earth, and should repaire
Our old decaies: who in such high esteeme,
Should prize all mortals, living in his feare;
As not to shun Death, Povertie, and Shame,
To save their soules, and spread his glorious Name.

And partly to fulfil his Fathers pleasure,
Whose powrefull hand allowes it not for strange,
If he vouchsafe the riches of his treasure,
Pure Righteousnesse to take such il exchange;
On all Iniquitie to make a seisure,
Giving his snow-white Weed for ours in change;
Our mortall garment in a skarlet Die,
Too base a roabe for Immortalitie.

Most happy news, that ever yet was brought,
When Poverty and Riches met together,
The wealth of Heaven, in our fraile clothing wrought
Salvation by his happy comming hither:
Mighty Messias, who so deerely bought
Us Slaves to sinne, farre lighter than a feather:
Toss'd to and fro with every wicked wind,
The world, the flesh, or Devill gives to blind.

Who on his shoulders our blacke sinnes doth beare
To that most blessed, yet accursed Crosse;
Where fastning them, he rids us of our feare,
Yea for our gaine he is content with losse,
Our ragged clothing scornes he not to weare,
Though foule, rent, torne, disgracefull, rough
and grosse,
Spunne by that monster Sinne, and weav'd by Shame,
Which grace it selfe, disgrac'd with impure blame.

How canst thou choose (faire Virgin) then but mourne,
When this sweet of-spring of thy body dies,
When thy faire eies beholds his bodie torne,
The peoples fury, heares the womens cries;
His holy name prophan'd, He made a scorne,
Abusde with all their hatefull slaunderous lies:
Bleeding and fainting in such wondrous sort,
As scarce his feeble limbes can him support.

Now Simon of Cyrene passeth them by,
Whom they compell sweet JESUS Crosse to beare
To Golgatha, there doe they meane to trie
All cruell meanes to worke in him dispaire:
That odious place, where dead mens skulls did lie,
There must our Lord for present death prepare:
His sacred blood must grace that loathsome field,
To purge more filth, than that foule place could yield.

For now arriv'd unto this hatefull place,
In which his Crosse erected needes must bee,
False hearts, and willing hands come on apace,
All prest to ill, and all desire to see:
Gracelesse themselves, still seeking to disgrace;
Bidding him, If the Sonne of God he bee,
To save himselfe, if he could others save,
With all th'opprobrious words that might deprave.

His harmelesse hands unto the Crosse they nailde,
And feet that never trode in sinners trace,
Betweene two theeves, unpitied, unbewailde,
Save of some few possessors of his grace,
With sharpest pangs and terrors thus appailde,
Sterne Death makes way, that Life might give him place:
His eyes with teares, his body full of wounds,
Death last of paines his sorrows all confounds.

His joynts dis-joynted, and his legges hang downe,
His alablaster breast, his bloody side,
His members torne, and on his head a Crowne
Of sharpest Thorns, to satisfie for pride:
Anguish and Paine doe all his Sences drowne,
While they his holy garments do divide:
His bowells drie, his heart full fraught with griefe,
Crying to him that yeelds him no reliefe.

This with the eie of Faith thou maist behold,
Deere Spouse of Christ, and more than I can write;
And here both Griefe and Joy thou maist unfold,
To view thy Love in this most heavy plight,
Bowing his head, his bloodlesse body cold;
Those eies waxe dimme that gave us all our light,
His count'nance pale, yet still continues sweet,
His blessed blood watring his pierced feet.

O glorious miracle without compare!
Last, but not least which was by him effected;
Uniting death, life, misery, joy and care,
By his sharpe passion in his deere elected:
Who doth the Badges of like Liveries weare,
Shall find how deere they are of him respected.
No joy, griefe, paine, life, death, was like to his,
Whose infinitie dolours wrought eternall blisse.

121

What creature on the earth did then remaine,
On whom the horror of this shamefull deed all creatures
Did not inflict some violent touch, or straine, at that
To see the Lord of all the world to bleed? instant when
His dying breath did rend huge rockes in twaine, Christ died.
The heavens betooke them to their mourning weed:
The Sunne grew darke, and scorn'd to give
them light,
Who durst ecclipse a glory farre more bright.

The Moone and Starres did hide themselves for shame,
The earth did tremble in her loyall feare,
The Temple vaile did rent to spread his fame,
The Monuments did open every where;
Dead Saints did rise forth of their graves, and came
To divers people that remained there
Within that holy City; whose offence,
Did put their Maker to this large expence.

Things reasonable, and reasonlesse possest
The terrible impression of this fact;
For his oppression made them all opprest,
When with his blood he seal'd so faire an act,
In restlesse miserie to procure our rest;
His glorious deedes that dreadfull prison sackt:
When Death, Hell, Divells, using all their powre,
Were overcome in that most blessed houre.

Being dead, he killed Death, and did survive
That prowd insulting Tyrant: in whose place
He sends bright Immortalitie to revive
Those whom his yron armes did long embrace;
Who from their loathsome graves brings them alive
In glory to behold their Saviours face:
Who tooke the keys of all Deaths powre away,
Opening to those that would his name obay.

O wonder, more than man can comprehend,
Our Joy and Griefe both at one instant fram'd,
Compounded: Contrarieties contend
Each to exceed, yet neither to be blam'd.
Our Griefe to see our Saviours wretched end,
Our Joy to know both Death and Hell he tam'd:
That we may say, O Death, where is thy sting?
Hell, yeeld thy victory to thy conq'ring King.

Can stony hearts refraine from shedding teares,
To view the life and death of this sweet Saint?
His austere course in yong and tender yeares,
When great indurements could not make him faint:
His wants, his paines, his torments, and his feares,
All which he undertooke without constraint,
To shew that infinite Goodnesse must restore,
What infinite Justice looked for, and more.

Yet, had he beene but of a meane degree,
His suffrings had beene small to what they were;
Meane minds will shew of what meane mouldes
they bee; 1235
Small griefes seeme great, yet Use doth make them beare:
But ah! tis hard to stirre a sturdy tree;
Great dangers hardly puts great minds in feare:
They will conceale their griefes which mightie grow
In their stout hearts untill they overflow.

If then an earthly Prince may ill endure
The least of those afflictions which he bare,
How could this all-commaunding King procure
Such grievous torments with his mind to square,
Legions of Angells being at his Lure?
He might have liv'd in pleasure without care:
None can conceive the bitter paines he felt,
When God and man must suffer without guilt.
Take all the Suffrings Thoughts can thinke upon,
In ev'ry man that this huge world hath bred;
Let all those Paines and Suffrings meet in one,
Yet are they not a Mite to that he did
Endure for us: Oh let us thinke thereon,
That God should have his pretious blood so shed:
His Greatnesse clothed in our fraile attire,
And pay so deare a ransome for the hire.

Loe, here was glorie, miserie, life and death,
An union of contraries did accord;
Gladnesse and sadnesse here had one berth,
This wonder wrought the Passion of our Lord,
He suffring for all the sinnes of all th'earth,
No satisfaction could the world afford:
But this rich Jewell, which from God was sent,
To call all those that would in time repent.

Which I present (deare Lady) to your view,
Upon the Crosse depriv'd of life or breath,
To judge if ever Lover were so true,
To yeeld himselfe unto such shamefull death:
Now blessed Joseph doth both beg and sue,
To have his body who possest his faith,
And thinkes, if he this small request obtaines,
He wins more wealth than in the world remaines.
Thus honourable Joseph is possest,
Of what his heart and soule so much desired,
And now he goes to give that body rest,
That all his life, with griefes and paines was tired;
He finds a Tombe, a Tombe most rarely blest,
In which was never creature yet interred;
There this most pretious body he incloses,
Imbalmd and deckt with Lillies and with Roses.

Loe here the Beautie of Heav'n and Earth is laid,
The purest coulers underneath the Sunne,
But in this place he cannot long be staid,
Glory must end what horror hath begun;
For he the furie of the Heavens obay'd,
And now he must possesse what he hath wonne:
The Maries doe with pretious balmes attend,
But beeing come, they find it to no end.

For he is rize from Death t'Eternall Life,
And now those pretious oyntments he desires
Are brought unto him, by his faithfull Wife
The holy Church; who in those rich attires,
Of Patience, Love, Long suffring, Voide of strife,
Humbly presents those oyntments he requires:
The oyles of Mercie, Charitie, and Faith,
Shee onely gives that which no other hath.

These pretious balmes doe heale his grievous wounds,
And water of Compunction washeth cleane
The soares of sinnes, which in our Soules abounds;
So faire it heales, no skarre is ever seene;
Yet all the glory unto Christ redounds, Canticles.
His pretious blood is that which must redeeme;
Those well may make us lovely in his sight,
But cannot save without his powrefull might.

This is that Bridegroome that appeares so faire,

So sweet, so lovely in his Spouses sight,
That unto Snowe we may his face compare,
His cheekes like skarlet, and his eyes so bright
As purest Doves that in the rivers are,
Washed with milke, to give the more delight;
His head is likened to the finest gold,
His curled lockes so beauteous to behold;

Blacke as a Raven in her blackest hew;
His lips like skarlet threeds, yet much more sweet
Than is the sweetest hony dropping dew,
Or hony combes, where all the Bees doe meet;
Yea, he is constant, and his words are true,
His cheekes are beds of spices, flowers sweet;
His lips like Lillies, dropping downe pure mirrhe,
Whose love, before all worlds we doe preferre.

Ah! give me leave (good Lady) now to leave
This taske of Beauty which I tooke in hand,
I cannot wade so deepe, I may deceave of Cumberland.
My selfe, before I can attaine the land;
Therefore (good Madame) in your heart I leave
His perfect picture, where it still shall stand,
Deepely engraved in that holy shrine,
Environed with Love and Thoughts divine.

There may you see him as a God in glory,
And as a man in miserable case;
There may you reade his true and perfect storie,
His bleeding body there you may embrace,
And kisse his dying cheekes with teares of sorrow,
With joyfull griefe, you may intreat for grace;
And all your prayers, and your almes-deeds
May bring to stop his cruell wounds that bleeds.

Oft times hath he made triall of your love,
And in your Faith hath tooke no small delight,
By Crosses and Afflictions he doth prove,
Yet still your heart remaineth firme and right;
Your love so strong, as nothing can remove,
Your thoughts beeing placed on him both day
and night,
Your constant soule doth lodge betweene her brests,
This Sweet of sweets, in which all glory rests.

Sometime h'appeares to thee in Shepheards weed,
And so presents himselfe before thine eyes,
A good old man; that goes his flocke to feed;
Thy colour changes, and thy heart doth rise;
Thou call'st, he comes, thou find'st tis he indeed,
Thy Soule conceaves that he is truely wise:
Nay more, desires that he may be the Booke,
Whereon thine eyes continually may looke.

Sometime imprison'd, naked, poore, and bare,
Full of diseases, impotent, and lame,
Blind, deafe, and dumbe, he comes unto his faire,
To see if yet shee will remaine the same;
Nay sicke and wounded, now thou do'st prepare
To cherish him in thy dear Lovers name:
Yea thou bestow'st all paines, all cost, all care,
That may relieve him, and his health repaire.

These workes of mercy are so sweete, so deare
To him that is the Lord of Life and Love,
That all thy prayers he vouchsafes to heare,
And sends his holy Spirit from above;
Thy eyes are op'ned, and thou seest so cleare,
No worldly thing can thy faire mind remove;
Thy faith, thy prayers, and his speciall grace
Doth open Heav'n, where thou behold'st his face.

These are those Keyes Saint Peter did possesse,
Which with a Spirituall powre are giv'n to thee,
To heale the soules of those that doe transgresse,
By thy faire virtues; which, if once they see,
Unto the like they doe their minds addresse,
Such as thou art, such they desire to be:
If they be blind, thou giv'st to them their sight;
If deafe or lame, they heare, and goe upright.

Yea, if possest with any evill spirits,
Such powre thy faire examples have obtain'd
To cast them out, applying Christs pure merits,
By which they are bound, and of all hurt restrain'd:
If strangely taken, wanting sence or wits,
Thy faith appli'd unto their soules so pain'd,
Healeth all griefes, and makes them grow so strong,
As no defects can hang upon them long.

Thou beeing thus rich, no riches do'st respect,
Nor do'st thou care for any outward showe;
The proud that doe faire Virtues rules neglect,
Desiring place, thou sittest them belowe:
All wealth and honour thou do'st quite reject,
If thou perceiv'st that once it prooves a foe
To virtue, learning, and the powres divine,
Thou mai'st convert, but never wilt incline

To fowle disorder, or licentiousnesse
But in thy modest vaile do'st sweetly cover
The staines of other sinnes, to make themselves,
That by this meanes thou mai'st in time recover
Those weake lost sheepe that did so long transgresse,
Presenting them unto thy deerest Lover;
That when he brings them backe unto his fold,
In their conversion then he may behold

Thy beauty shining brighter than the Sunne,
Thine honour more than ever Monarke gaind,
Thy wealth exceeding his that Kingdomes wonne,
Thy Love unto his Spouse, thy Faith unfaind,
Thy Constancy in what thou hast begun,
Till thou his heavenly Kingdom have obtaind;
Respecting worldly wealth to be but drosse,
Which, if abuz'd, doth proove the owners losse.

Great Cleopatra's love to Anthony,
Can no way be compared unto thine;
Shee left her Love in his extremitie,
When greatest need should cause her to combine
Her force with his, to get the Victory:
Her Love was earthly, and thy Love Divine;
Her Love was onely to support her pride,
Humilitie thy Love and Thee doth guide.

That glorious part of Death, which last shee plai'd,
T'appease the ghost of her deceased Love,
Had never needed, if shee could have stai'd
When his extreames made triall, and did prove
Her leaden love unconstant, and afraid:
Their wicked warres the wrath of God might move
To take revenge for chast Octavia's wrongs,
Because shee enjoyes what unto her belongs.

No Cleopatra, though thou wert as faire
As any Creature in Antonius eyes;
Yea though thou wert as rich, as wise, as rare,
As any Pen could write, or Wit devise;
Yet with this Lady canst thou not compare,
Whose inward virtues all thy worth denies:
Yet thou a blacke Egyptian do'st appeare;
Thou false, shee true; and to her Love more deere.

Shee sacrificeth to her deerest Love,
With flowres of Faith, and garlands of Good deeds;
Shee flies not from him when afflictions prove,
Shee beares his crosse, and stops his wounds that bleeds;
Shee love and lives chaste as the Turtle dove,
Shee attends upon him, and his flocke shee feeds;
Yea for one touch of death which thou did'st trie,
A thousand deaths shee every day doth die.

Her virtuous life exceeds thy worthy death,
Yea, she hath richer ornaments of state,
Shining more glorious than in dying breath
Thou didst; when either pride, or cruell fate,
Did worke thee to prevent a double death;
To stay the malice, scorne, and cruell hate
Of Rome; that joy'd to see thy pride pull'd downe,
Whose Beauty wrought the hazard of her Crowne.

Good Madame, though your modestie be such,
Not to acknowledge what we know and find;
And that you thinke these prayses overmuch,
Which doe expresse the beautie of your mind;
Yet pardon me although I give a touch
Unto their eyes, that else would be so blind,
As not to see thy store, and their owne wants
From whose faire seeds of Virtue spring
these plants.

And knowe, when first into this world I came,
This charge was giv'n me by th'Eternall powres,
Th'everlasting Trophie of thy fame,
To build and decke it with the sweetest flowres
That virtue yeelds; Then Madame, doe not blame
Me, when I shew the World but what is yours,
And decke you with that crowne which is your due,
That of Heav'ns beauty Earth may take a view.

Though famous women elder times have knowne,
Whose glorious actions did appeare so bright,
That powrefull men by them were overthrowne,
And all their armies overcome in fight;
The Scythian women by their powre alone,
Put king Darius unto shamefull flight:
All Asia yeelded to their conq'ring hand,
Great Alexander could not their powre withstand.

Whose worth, though writ in lines of blood and fire,
Is not to be compared unto thine;
Their powre was small to overcome Desire,
Or to direct their wayes by Virtues line:
Were they alive, they would thy Life admire,
And unto thee their honours would resigne:
For thou a greater conquest do'st obtaine,
Than they who have so many thousands slaine.

Wise Deborah that judged Israel,
Nor valiant Judeth cannot equall thee,
Unto the first, God did his will reveale,
And gave her powre to set his people free;
Yea Judeth had the powre likewise to queale
Proud Holifernes, that the just might see
What small defence vaine pride, and greatnesse hath
Against the weapons of Gods word and faith.

But thou farre greater warre do'st still maintaine,
Against that many headed monster Sinne,
Whose mortall sting hath many thousand slaine,
And every day fresh combates doe begin;
Yet cannot all his venome lay one staine
Upon thy Soule, thou do'st the conquest winne,
Though all the world he daily doth devoure,
Yet over thee he never could get powre.

For that one worthy deed by Deb'rah done,
Thou hast performed many in thy time;
For that one Conquest that faire Judeth wonne,
By which shee did the steps of honour clime;
Thou hast the Conquest of all Conquests wonne,
When to thy Conscience Hell can lay no crime:
For that one head that Judeth bare away,
Thou tak'st from Sinne a hundred heads a day.

129

Though virtuous Hester fasted three dayes space,
And spent her time in prayers all that while,
That by Gods powre shee might obtaine such grace,
That shee and hers might not become a spoyle
To wicked Hamon, in whose crabbed face
Was seene the map of malice, envie, guile;
Her glorious garments though shee put apart,
So to present a pure and single heart
To God, in sack-cloth, ashes, and with teares;
Yet must faire Hester needs give place to thee,
Who hath continu'd dayes, weekes, months,
and yeares,
In Gods true service, yet thy heart beeing free
From doubt of death, or any other feares:
Fasting from sinne, thou pray'st thine eyes may see
Him that hath full possession of thine heart,
From whose sweet love thy Soule can never part.

His Love, not Feare, makes thee to fast and pray,
No kinsmans counsell needs thee to advise;
The sack-cloth thou do'st weare both night and day,
Is worldly troubles, which thy rest denies;
The ashes are the Vanities that play
Over thy head, and steale before thine eyes;
Which thou shak'st off when mourning time is past,
That royall roabes thou may'st put on at last.

Joachims wife; that faire and constant Dame,
Who rather chose a cruel death to die,
Than yeeld to those two Elders voide of shame,
When both at once her chastitie did trie,
Whose Innocencie bare away the blame,
Untill th'Almighty Lord had heard her crie;
And rais'd the spirit of a Child to speake,
Making the powrefull judged of the weake.

Although her virtue doe deserve to be
Writ by that hand that never purchas'd blame;
In holy Writ, where all the world may see
Her perfit life, and ever honoured name:
Yet was she not to be compar'd to thee,
Whose many virtues doe increase thy fame:
For shee oppos'd against old doting Lust,
Who with lifes danger she did feare to trust.

But your chaste breast, guarded with strength of mind,
Hates the imbracements of unchaste desires;
You loving God, live in your selfe confind
From unpure Love, your purest thoughts retires,
Your perfit sight could never be so blind,
To entertaine the old or yong desires
Of idle Lovers; which the world presents,
Whose base abuses worthy minds prevents.

Even as the constant Lawrell, alwayes greene,
No parching heate of Summer can deface,
Nor pinching Winter ever yet was seene,
Whose nipping frosts could wither, or disgrace:
So you (deere Ladie) still remaine as Queene,
Subduing all affections that are base,
Unalterable by the change of times,
Not following, but lamenting others crimes.

No feare of Death, or dread of open shame,
Hinders your perfect heart to give consent;
Nor loathsome age, whom Time could never tame
From ill designes, whereto their youth was bent;
But love of God, care to preserve your fame,
And spend that pretious time that God hath sent,
In all good exercises of the minde,
Whereto your noble nature is inclin'd.

That Ethyopian Queene did gaine great fame,
Who from the Southerne world, did come to see
Great Salomon; the glory of whose name
Had spread it selfe ore all the earth, to be
So great, that all the Princes thither came,
To be spectators of his royaltie:
And this faire Queene of Sheba came from farre,
To reverence this new appearing starre.

From th'utmost part of all the Earth shee came,
To heare the Wisdom of this worthy King;
To trie if Wonder did agree with Fame,
And many faire rich presents did she bring:
Yea many strange hard questions did shee frame,
All which were answer'd by this famous King:
Nothing was hid that in her heart did rest,
And all to proove this King so highly blest.

131

Here Majestie with Majestie did meete,
Wisdome to Wisdome yeelded true content,
One Beauty did another Beauty greet,
Bountie to Bountie never could repent;
Here all distaste is troden under feet,
No losse of time, where time was so well spent
In virtuous exercises of the minde,
In which this Queene did much contentment finde.

Spirits affect where they doe sympathize,
Wisdom desires Wisdome to embrace,
Virtue covets her like, and doth devize
How she her friends may entertaine with grace;
Beauty sometime is pleas'd to feed her eyes,
With viewing Beautie in anothers face:
Both good and bad in this point doe agree,
That each desireth with his like to be.

And this Desire did worke a strange effect,
To drawe a Queene forth of her native Land,
Not yeelding to the nicenesse and respect
Of woman-kind; shee past both sea and land,
All feare of dangers shee did quite neglect,
Onely to see, to heare, and understand
That beauty, wisedome, majestie, and glorie,
That in her heart imprest his perfect storie.

Yet this faire map of majestie and might,
Was but a figure of thy deerest Love,
Borne t'expresse that true and heavenly light,
That doth all other joyes imperfect prove;
If this faire Earthly starre did shine so bright,
What doth that glorious Sonne that is above?
Who weares th'imperiall crowne of heaven
and earth,
And made all Christians blessed in his berth.

If that small sparke could yeeld so great a fire,
As to inflame the hearts of many Kings
To come to see, to heare, and to admire
His wisdome, tending but to worldly things;
Then much more reason have we to desire
That heav'nly wisedome, which salvation brings;
The Sonne of righteousnesse, that gives true joyes,
When all they fought for, were but Earthly toyes.

No travels ought th'affected soule to shunne,
That this faire heavenly Light desires to see:
This King of kings to whom we all should runne,
To view his Glory and his Majestie;
He without whom we all had beene undone,
He that from Sinne and Death hath set us free,
And overcome Satan, the world, and sinne,
That by his merits we those joyes might winne.

Prepar'd by him, whose everlasting throne
Is plac'd in heaven, above the starrie skies,
Where he that sate, was like the Jasper stone,
Who rightly knowes him shall be truely wise,
A Rainebow round about his glorious throne;
Nay more, those winged beasts so full of eies,
That never cease to glorifie his Name,
Who was, and will be, and is now the same.

This is that great almightie Lord that made
Both heaven and earth, and lives for evermore;
By him the worlds foundation first was laid:
He fram'd the things that never were before:
The Sea within his bounds by him is staid,
He judgeth all alike, both rich and poore:
All might, all majestie, all love, all lawe
Remaines in him that keepes all worlds in awe.

From his eternall throne the lightning came,
Thundrings and Voyces did from thence proceede;
And all the creatures glorifi'd his name,
In heaven, in earth, and seas, they all agreed,
When loe that spotlesse Lambe so voyd of blame,
That for us di'd, whose sinnes did make him bleed:
That true Physition that so many heales,
Opened the Booke, and did undoe the Seales.

He onely worthy to undoe the Booke
Of our charg'd soules, full of iniquitie,
Where with the eyes of mercy he doth looke
Upon our weakenesse and infirmitie;
This is that corner stone that was forsooke,
Who leaves it, trusts but to uncertaintie:
This is Gods Sonne, in whom he is well pleased,
His deere beloved, that his wrath appeased.

He that had powre to open all the Seales,
And summon up our sinnes of blood and wrong,
He unto whom the righteous soules appeales,
That have bin martyrd, and doe thinke it long,
To whom in mercie he his will reveales,
That they should rest a little in their wrong,
Untill their fellow servants should be killed,
Even as they were, and that they were fulfilled.

Pure thoughted Lady, blessed be thy choyce
Of this Almightie, everlasting King;
In thee his Saints and Angels doe rejoyce,.
And to their Heav'nly Lord doe daily sing
Thy perfect praises in their lowdest voyce;
And all their harpes and golden vials bring
Full of sweet odours, even thy holy prayers
Unto that spotlesse Lambe, that all repaires.
Of whom that Heathen Queene obtain'd such grace,
By honouring but the shadow of his Love,
That great Judiciall day to have a place,
Condemning those that doe unfaithfull prove;
Among the haplesse, happie is her case,
That her deere Saviour spake for her behove;
And that her memorable Act should be
Writ by the hand of true Eternitie.

Yet this rare Phoenix of that worne-out age,
This great majesticke Queene comes short of thee
Who to an earthly Prince did then ingage
Her hearts desires, her love, her libertie,
Acting her glorious part upon a Stage
Of weaknesse, frailtie, and infirmity:
Giving all honour to a Creature, due
To her Creator, whom shee never knew.

But loe, a greater thou hast sought and found
Than Salomon in all his royaltie;
And unto him thy faith most firmely bound
To serve and honour him continually;
That glorious God, whose terror doth confound
All sinfull workers of iniquitie:
Him hast thou truely served all thy life,
And for his love, liv'd with the world at strife.
To this great Lord, thou onely art affected,

Yet came he not in pompe or royaltie,
But in an humble habit, base, dejected;
A King, a God, clad in mortalitie,
He hath thy love, thou art by him directed,
His perfect path was faire humilitie:
Who being Monarke of heav'n, earth, and seas,
Indur'd all wrongs, yet no man did displease.

Then how much more art thou to be commended,
That seek'st thy love in lowly shepheards weed?
A seeming Trades-mans sonne, of none attended,
Save of a few in povertie and need;
Poore Fishermen that on his love attended,
His love that makes so many thousands bleed:
Thus did he come, to trie our faiths the more,
Possessing worlds, yet seeming extreame poore.

The Pilgrimes travels, and the Shepheards cares,
He tooke upon him to enlarge our soules,
What pride hath lost, humilitie repaires,
For by his glorious death he us inroules
In deepe Characters, writ with blood and teares,
Upon those blessed Everlasting scroules;
His hands, his feete, his body, and his face,
Whence freely flow'd the rivers of his grace.

Sweet holy rivers, pure celestiall springs,
Proceeding from the fountaine of our life;
Swift sugred currents that salvation brings,
Cleare christall streames, purging all sinne and strife,
Faire floods, where souls do bathe their snow-white
wings,
Before they flie to true eternall life:
Sweet Nectar and Ambrosia, food of Saints,
Which, whoso tasteth, never after faints.

This hony dropping dew of holy love,
Sweet milke, wherewith we weaklings are restored,
Who drinkes thereof, a world can never move,
All earthly pleasures are of them abhorred;
This love made Martyrs many deaths to prove,
To taste his sweetnesse, whom they so adored:
Sweetnesse that makes our flesh a burthen to us,
Knowing it serves but onely to undoe us.

135

His sweetnesse sweet'ned all the sowre of death,
To faithfull Stephen his appointed Saint;
Who by the river stones did loose his breath,
When paines nor terrors could not make him faint:
So was this blessed Martyr turn'd to earth,
To glorifie his soule by deaths attaint:
This holy Saint was humbled and cast downe,
To winne in heaven an everlasting crowne.

Whose face repleat with Majestie and Sweetnesse,
Did as an Angel unto them appeare,
That sate in Counsell hearing his discreetnesse,
Seeing no change, or any signe of a feare;
But with a constant browe did there confesse
Christs high deserts, which were to him so deare:
Yea when these Tyrants stormes did most oppresse,
Christ did appeare to make his griefe the lesse.

For beeing filled with the holy Ghost,
Up unto Heav'n he look'd with stedfast eies,
Where God appeared with his heavenly hoste
In glory to this Saint before he dies;
Although he could no Earthly pleasures boast,
At Gods right hand sweet JESUS he espies;
Bids them behold Heavens open, he doth see
The Sonne of Man at Gods right hand to be.

Whose sweetnesse sweet'ned that short sowre of Life,
Making all bitternesse delight his taste,
Yeelding sweet quietnesse in bitter strife,
And most contentment when he di'd disgrac'd;
Heaping up joyes where sorrows were most rife;
Such sweetnesse could not choose but be imbrac'd:
The food of Soules, the Spirits onely treasure,
The Paradise of our celestiall pleasure.

This Lambe of God, who di'd, and was alive,
Presenting us the bread of life Eternall,
His bruised body powrefull to revive
Our sinking soules, out of the pit infernall;
For by this blessed food he did contrive
A worke of grace, by this his gift externall,
With heav'nly Manna, food of his elected,
To feed their soules, of whom he is respected.

This wheate of Heaven the blessed Angells bread,
Wherewith he feedes his deere adopted Heires;
Sweet foode of life that doth revive the dead,
And from the living takes away all cares;
To taste this sweet Saint Laurence did not dread,
The broyling gridyorne cool'd with holy teares:
Yeelding his naked body to the fire,
To taste this sweetnesse, such was his desire.

Nay, what great sweetnesse did th'Apostles taste,
Condemn'd by Counsell, when they did returne;
Rejoycing that for him they di'd disgrac'd,
Whose sweetnes made their hearts and soules so burne
With holy zeale and love most pure and chaste;
For him they sought from whome they might not turne:
Whose love made Andrew goe most joyfully,
Unto the Crosse, on which he meant to die.

The Princes of th'Apostles were so filled
With the delicious sweetnes of his grace,
That willingly they yeelded to be killed,
Receiving deaths that were most vile and base,
For his name sake, that all might be fulfilled.
They with great joy all torments did imbrace:
The ugli'st face that Death could ever yeeld,
Could never feare these Champions from the field.

They still continued in their glorious fight,
Against the enemies of flesh and blood;
And in Gods law did set their whole delight,
Suppressing evill, and erecting good:
Not sparing Kings in what they did not right,
Their noble Actes they seal'd with deerest blood:
One chose the Gallowes, that unseemely death,
The other by the Sword did loose his breath.

His Head did pay the dearest rate of sin,
Yeelding it joyfully unto the Sword,
To be cut off as he had never bin,
For speaking truth according to Gods word,
Telling king Herod of incestuous sin,
That hatefull crime of God and man abhorr'd:
His brothers wife, that prowd licentious Dame,
Cut off his Head to take away his shame.

Loe Madame, heere you take a view of those,
Whose worthy steps you doe desire to tread,
Deckt in those colours which our Saviour chose;
The purest colours both of White and Red, Colours of
Their freshest beauties would I faine disclose, Confessors
By which our Saviour most was honoured:
But my weake Muse desireth now to rest,
Folding up all their Beauties in your breast.

Whose excellence hath rais'd my sprites to write,
Of what my thoughts could hardly apprehend;
Your rarest Virtues did my soule delight,
Great Ladie of my heart: I must commend
You that appeare so faire in all mens sight:
On your Deserts my Muses doe attend:
You are the Articke Starre that guides my hand,
All what I am, I rest at your command.

TO THE DOUBTFULL READER

Gentle Reader, if thou desire to be resolued, why I
giue this Title, Salue Deus Rex Judaeorum, know
for certaine, that it was deliuered vnto me in sleepe
many yeares before I had any intent to write in this
maner, and was quite out of my memory vntill I had written
the Passion of Christ, when immediately it came into my re-
membrance, what I had dreamed long before; and thinking
it a significant token, that I was appointed to performe that
Worke, I gaue the very same words I receiued in sleepe as the
fittest Title I could deuise for this Booke.

TO ALL VERTUOUS LADIES IN GENERALL

Each blessed Lady that in Virtue spends
Your pretious time to beautifie your soules;
Come wait on hir whom winged Fame attends
And in hir hand the Booke where she inroules
Those high deserts that Maiestie commends:
Let this faire Queene not unattended bee
When in my Glasse she daines her selfe to see.

Put on your wedding garments euery one,
The Bridegroome stayes to entertaine you all;
Let Virtue be your guide, for she alone

Can leade you right that you can neuer fall;
And make no stay for feare he should be gone:
But fill your Lamps with oyle of burning zeale,
That to your Faith he may his Truth reueale.

The roabes
that Christ
wore before
his death.

Let all your roabes be purple scarlet white,
Those perfit colours purest Virtue wore,
Come deckt with Lillies that did so delight
To be preferr'd in Beauty, farre before
Wise Salomon in all his glory dight:
Whose royall roabes did no such pleasure yield,
As did the beauteous Lilly of the field.

In token of
Constancie.

Adorne your temples with faire Daphnes crowne,
The neuer changing Laurel, alwaies greene;
Let constant hope all worldly pleasures drowne,
In wise Mineruaes paths be alwaies seene;
Or with bright Cynthia, thogh faire Venus frown:
With Esop crosse the posts of euery doore,
Where Sinne would riot, making Virtue poore.

And let the Muses your companions be,
Those sacred sisters that on Pallas wait,
Whose Virtues with the purest minds agree,
Whose godly labours doe auoyd the baite
Of worldly pleasures, liuing alwaies free
From sword, from violence, and from ill report,
To those nine Worthies all faire mindes resort.

Annoynt your haire with Aarons pretious oyle,
And bring your palmes of vict'ry in your hands,
To ouercome all thoughts that would defile
The earthly circuit of your soules faire lands;

139

Let no dimme shadowes your cleare eyes beguile:
Sweet odours, mirrhe, gum, aloes, frankincense,
Present that King who di'd for your offence.

Behold, bright Titans shining chariot staies,
All deckt with flowers of the freshest hew,
Attended on by Age, Houres, Nights, and Daies,
Which alters not your beauty, but giues you
Much more, and crownes you with eternall praise:
This golden chariot wherein you must ride,
Let simple Doues, and subtill serpents guide.

Come swifter than the motions of the Sunne,
To be transfigur'd with our louing Lord,
Lest Glory end what Grace in you begun,
Of heau'nly riches make your greatest hoord,
In Christ all honour, wealth, and beautie's wonne:
By whose perfections you appeare more faire
Than Phoebus, if he seau'n times brighter were.

Gods holy Angels will direct your Doues,
And bring your Serpents to the fields of rest,
Where he doth stay that purchast all your loues
In bloody torments, when he di'd opprest,
There shall you find him in those pleasant groues
Of sweet Elizium, by the Well of Life,
Whose cristal springs do purge from worldly strife

Thus may you flie from dull and sensuall earth,
Whereof at first your bodies formed were,
That new regen'rate in a second berth,
Your blessed soules may liue without all feare,
Beeing immortall, subject to no death:
But in the eie of heauen so highly placed,
That others by your virtues may be graced.

Where worthy Ladies I will leaue you all,
Desiring you to grace this little Booke;
Yet some of you me thinkes I heare to call
Me by my name, and bid me better looke,
Lest unawares I in an error fall:
In generall tearmes, to place you with the rest,
Whom Fame commends to be the very best.

Tis true, I must confesse (O noble Fame)
There are a number honoured by thee,
Of which, some few thou didst recite by name,
And willd my Muse they should remembred bee;
Wishing some would their glorious Trophies frame:
Which if I should presume to undertake,
My tired Hand for very feare would quake.

Onely by name I will bid some of those,
That in true Honors seate haue long bin placed,
Yea euen such as thou hast chiefly chose,
By whom my Muse may be the better graced;
Therefore, unwilling longer time to lose,
I will inuite some Ladies that I know,
But chiefly those as thou hast graced so.

WWW.OBERONBOOKS.COM

Follow us on Twitter @oberonbooks
& Facebook @OberonBooksLondon